My Sister and I

Survivors of Rape and Incest

My Sister and I

Survivors of Rape and Incest

The True-life Story of two sisters
Deena and Starla,
sexual victims at the ages of 4 and 5

As told to:
J. Jackson Owensby

A-Argus Better Book Publishers, LLC
North Carolina ~ * ~ ~ * ~ New Jersey

My Sister and I
Survivors of Rape and Incest

The Rape, Sodomy and Sexual Molestation of Deena, age 4 and Starla age 5

The True-Life Story of Deena and Starla
As told to: J. Jackson Owensby

All Rights Reserved © 2008
By: Argus Enterprises International, Inc.

No part of this book may be reproduced or transmitted in any form or by any means, mechanical, graphic, electronic, or including photocopying, recording, taping, or by any information storage retrieval system, without the permission in writing from the publisher.

A-Argus Better Book Publishers, LLC
For Information:
Argus Enterprises International, Inc.
P O Box 914
Kernersville, NC 27284
www.a-argusbooks.com

ISBN: 0-9801555-3-3
ISBN: 978-0-9801555-3-2

Book Cover designed by Dubya

Printed in the United States of America

~ Dedication ~

This book is dedicated to every little one who lives, or has lived, with this. Know that I believe you and that you are not alone. It's not your fault and it never was. I made it out and you can, too.

Thanks for being brave enough to do this, Pop. Love ya!

Deena

~ Thank You ~

To merely say 'thank you' to you, Deena and to you, Starla for the privilege of putting your story to paper seems insignificant compared to the trauma you both lived and the difficulty each of you have had in relating the horrific experiences that you lived through. Still, your courage in exposing such a dire situation may just help some uncertain politician move a little faster in putting into place tough laws that will rid society of such animals, as permeated the lives of two innocent children. Still, the only thing that I can think of to say to you on behalf of all of the little children who have experienced, and who are right now undergoing similar dastardly acts by evil men and women, is that your courage is most appreciated.

Would that there were many others so courageous. Perhaps we could stop this.

J.J.O

~ Introduction ~

"Can you imagine yourself being a four-year-old baby girl, sitting naked on a kitchen countertop with your step-daddy's sticky, gooey semen all over your face, your body, your hands, and in your hair and your mouth?"

With those terrible words, Deena, my future daughter-in-law began to describe the sexual horrors visited on her at the innocent age of four, and her sister, Starla, who was only five years old, continuing throughout the rest of their childhood and beyond.

How did it all start?

~ * ~

"Pop, would you write my story?"

The question came out of nowhere.

I had been sitting at my desk, leaning back in my chair, contemplating the fate of the universe. Yeah, right!

Okay, so I had my eyes closed while I was contemplating. I really wasn't asleep, at least not completely but I had been lost somewhere out there.

The question began to soak in and my brain began to awaken. My future daughter-in-law had asked me an interesting question. And as it turns out, it was a lulu of a question.

Write her story? What story? Why would she ask that of me? I had never really considered myself a real author, although I had long wanted to write novels. And in fact, I was lucky enough to even have written one book that was just being published.

It had been my first serious attempt at trying to have a manuscript published, and to my shock and surprise, a publisher had agreed to issue the book. Would you believe on my first attempt? Do you know how rare that occurrence is? Especially when there are literally hundreds of thousands of better-than-I writers submitting manuscripts every day? Such a feat is virtually unheard of, especially when you realize that this writer is not proficient with words, his spelling is atrocious, his punctuation is worse and his grammar is straight out of the hills of his bucolic upbringing.

Despite these handicaps of mine and even with her number one editor screaming, "Save me from this animal!" a feisty, semi-young publisher from New Jersey decided that my story about the abuse a young homosexual man from Indiana was suffering at the hands of the federal authorities merited a look and possibly exposure. It must have been the theme; it couldn't possibly have been the author. That same publisher urged me to continue writing.

Boy! Talk about an ego booster.

Deena, my oldest son's fiancé, had been a proofreader of '*Deliberate Indifference: A Gay Man's Maltreatment by the United States Department of Justice*', the title of the one book that I had published. She had frequently made comments about the courage of a gay young man willing to reveal his entire life's troubles in the hopes that the abuse by the authorities that he was suffering would ease, but more in the hopes that the consistent and flagrant abusive practices by the Federal Bureau of Prison authorities and employees that affected thousands of inmates could be brought to light.

But, this was different. I looked at Deena, and she could read the question in my eyes.

"I was sexually abused when I was four years old," she said. Her tears began to flow, her voice cracked and broke as she sobbed, but she found the strength to continue. "Raped or sodomized almost every day by my stepfather and by my stepbrothers, and then by their friends. So was at least one of my older sisters, Starla, who was only five when it started with her. All the while my mother stood by and did nothing to protect us. And he—that bastard, that cruel, inhuman bastard—is still out there. I, we, want you to help us protect other young and innocent children."

I'm not sure that I will ever be able to find words that will convey the feeling and depth of the emotional shock that ran through me at those words, delivered with so much apparent agony for the speaker.

Noticing the look of astonishment on my face, Deena broke into tears, weeping and sobbing. While my mind told me that this was a story that I really, really didn't want to hear, my primitive instincts told me that I must listen. The feeling of outrage that had driven me to write the story about Chris Wehner was nothing compared to the building tide of fury that was beginning to cloud my vision.

Comforting the weeping young woman the best that I could, I assured her that I would be glad to listen and then help expose the villain or villains, if it were in my power.

Once Deena had begun to relate her life story a magical moment happened. Starla, one of Deena's sisters, also opened herself up and decided that she would be willing to contribute her side of the story as well. This was something most amazing;

something that had never happened before. Starla had always refused even to just talk about the sordid events that took place while she was a child. She wouldn't even speak of the events to other members of her family. Not even to her sisters or other female relatives or friends.

Why Starla relented and agreed to speak with me and also agreed to relate equally disturbing experiences, I'll never know. Perhaps it was just that the time was right. Or perhaps, it may have been that Deena had led the way.

What follows now is exposure of the sexual rape of two young girls, babies, starting virtually at the age of infancy and continuing into their teen-age years. Not just once, but on and on and on—over and over.

Rape.

Sodomy.

Incest.

Fellatio.

If there's a name for it, it happened. This is a tale filled with horror and pain, tears and sorrow, degradation and depravity. It is an extremely difficult tale to put to paper and it will be an upsetting tale for the reader to read, as it will expose the true evil of man; men who prey on young children, men who prey on the helpless, men who prey on their own family. It's a side of mankind that lurks in the shadows; an evil that we don't even want to admit exists. But it is there—in reality.

A sudden uncomfortable thought jarred my consciousness, as I sit here trying to determine where to begin. How can I possibly describe the depth of the horror and terror that these valiant young women introduced to me?

What the hell am I doing writing this genre of a book? It's certainly not the type of story I long dreamed of writing. Sure, I had made the decision that I wanted to be a writer, to be an author. I wanted to write to entertain or be amusing, a la Louis L'Amour or Dan Brown, or perhaps, Robert

Ludlum. Even one of a hundred other mind-grabbing authors. Write an interesting, thrilling novel or series, find a large publisher and get rich. Every writer's dream. Right!

But, this? This was beyond my wildest imagination. Then, why me?

After all, I am most certainly not a crusading do-gooder, out to make everything right in the world. And I'm definitely no angel myself. But, for the second time in a relatively short span of my life, I have been brought face to face with a situation that shrieks to be exposed, an evil that cries out for vengeance; despicable and vile degradation that must be unveiled for all to witness.

The situation?

Rape—repeated, over and over continuously, never-ending vicious rape of a four-year old baby and of a five-year old infant.

Oh, sure! Be nice. Be politically correct. Don't offend the monsters. Call it 'Sexual Molestation.' That doesn't make it sound so vile, so harsh. Or, name it 'incest.' After all, it's in the family. Even 'sexual activity.' That's politically correct. Pedophilia.

A lot of fancy names, but deep down, where it gets real dirty, it's still rape. Pure and simple, brutal and raw:

Physical, forceful carnal sex with a baby and a child by adults—grown men. Even worse, raped by their stepfather, as well by their stepbrothers. Raped and molested also by friends and acquaintances of the family. And that's just the beginning of the list.

Can you imagine the shock, the horror, the confusion, the terror, and the dread that has to eat at the nubile minds of a four-year-old infant and a five-year-old child who became the sexual targets of a maniacal stepfather and their stepbrothers, not to again mention by their cronies? And others—strangers?

Not once, nor twice, but day after day after terrible day and nights. And it went on for years. Not one year, not even two, but many, many years, with no one available to ease the pain, the grief, the anguish. Not one person No one to soften the agony, to assuage the torture that assaulted these children's minds and young bodies. No one to explain why an adult would visit such vile actions on two innocents. Not even a loving, caring mother.

~ * ~

If you have been watching television in recent years, it's probable that you have heard Bill O'Reilly's often-stated tirade regarding Jessica's Law, and the need for it to be adopted by every state to help protect the innocent. A law that is designed to punish the sexual perverts; to eliminate the predators, or at least to put them away for a very long time; and also those who just stand by while a child is badly used. It is a much-needed piece of legislature.

God, but how badly it is needed. However, that doesn't address the entire story. It doesn't touch the most heinous of crimes: incest.

Nor does the media help. It's easy to sit uninvolved, remaining emotionally calm, and read a newspaper or hear a television news program and learn that yet another adult has been arrested for child molestation. In fact, it is rare that a day goes by when at least one or more such story doesn't get reported. In the great state of North Carolina alone, in the first two and one-half months of this year, there has already been stories about adults being arrested for the rape of a ten-year old girl in Onslow County; the rape of a thirteen-year old girl by two men in Black Mountain; the rape of a ten-year old girl in Buncombe County; the rape of a nine-year old girl in Wilmington; the rape of a fourteen-year old girl in Burlington; the drugging and rape of one ten-year old girl and twelve-year old girl in Lexington; the rape of a seven-year old girl in Hickory; the rape of two ten-year old girls in Albemarle; the rape of an eight-year old girl by her mother's boyfriend in Catawba County; the rape of a six-year old girl in Jacksonville; and the rape of a fifteen-year old step-daughter by a man in Durham.

Are you surprised at the amazingly huge number of sexual molestation and rapes that are being reported? Then, you will be absolutely stunned by the fact that *less than five percent* of all the sexual molestations that occur are ever reported. That's right! **Less than five percent!** Did you know that the majority of the rape or molestation cases that are never reported are committed by a family member—often by a father, or stepfather, by a brother, or a stepbrother, and less frequently, by a mother or a sister or an aunt.

And, in many (even most) instances, fear of retaliation or the fear of the shame or embarrassment keeps other members of the family from exposing the molestation. These members are often persuaded that the public exposure of such a crime is a stain or stigma on the entire family.

B.S.

Wake up, damn it! And, yes. I mean you!

Have I caught your attention? Are you sitting there, reading this in the warm security of your own world, wondering what this blazing outrage is all about? Has the constant outpouring of negative media brought you to a state of emotional numbness that will allow you to become aware of these statistics and still remain somewhat aloof?

Well, so was I.

At least, I remained remote from it all until it came closer to home. In my own family! Or at least, what is soon to become my family, as I learned of the unbelievable childhood tortures that my future daughter-in-law and her sister had experienced. Hearing only the first few vague details caused me to choke with rage. Rage because, in this great country that has been freely given to us, there are a considerable number of despicable individuals who, for whatever reason, deliberately prey on the young, the innocent, the defenseless. And, for the most part, we—you and I, the public—just casually read about the situation. Then we just go ahead and play golf, enjoy the theatre or partake of a fine meal.

For me, that attitude has changed. My emotions have been touched. No, not touched—assaulted; flailed. And, as I write these words, it is difficult to keep those emotions under control. Had these events occurred in the mountains where I spent my childhood, the perpetrators would not have survived. He, she or they would have been shot or lynched.

Sure, many of my mountain-bred ancestors married young. But there was a marriage, agreed to by the parents if not the children. There existed no such vileness, as that which is often only a commonplace matter of form today, so easily ignored by a non-caring and uninvolved public. Or softened by pleasant sounding names created by well meaning psychoanalyst's efforts to describe what is truly monstrous behavior. This is a most evil behavior that must be brought to an end—now.

Once, I believed in the death penalty. Kill the low-life! Let God have them. In fact, as jury foreman, I once voted for a vicious human being to be executed. My views have changed, as I believe that for certain sadistic individuals, an easy death is much too forgiving. Saddam Hussein didn't suffer nearly enough.

Punishment for this sexually perverted type of individual should not be terminated so abruptly, but should go on for decades, if not eternity. And it should be the worst imaginable; locked into some hellhole, such as solitary confinement—hidden away from all human contact.

Such monsters' lives should be a continuing, fiery eternal hell such as they have created for their innocent victims. And I would vote to do everything we could to keep them alive as long as we could so that they could continue to suffer.

The 'Good Book' says that we should forgive and love our neighbors. As hard as that is, when you consider Hitler, Stalin, Genghis Khan, and Attila the Hun, I do try. But these evil people?

Forgiving an individual might be possible, perhaps, but not his or her sadistic actions. Certainly, not in the evil that has been visited upon my son's future wife and her sister, and upon the hundreds of thousands of children that have no advocate. May a loving God watch over these young infants and may a caring public awaken to their danger.

~ * ~

This manuscript is not undertaken with any great sense of happiness, only with a feeling of impending disgust with mankind. In fact, I'd rather not put these horrific words down on paper and expose these women and my family to the public mortification that will certainly occur. This declaration is certainly an indictment of society at large, and I am a part of that society.

In addition, I know that I will hear and will learn things from these women that I would rather not imagine that any one human being is willing to do to another human being, especially young, innocent, children. Emotions that I don't want to surface will be felt. Tears will be shed for the anguish that these two children experienced; but my tears will be nothing like the tears that the young victims, and others like them, have wept.

And, as hard as it will be for me to listen and to write the words, it will be much worse for the women to tell.

As difficult as it is for the two women to talk about the evil actions that only deranged and vile beings could cause to happen to the innocent, Deena and Starla know that out there in the real world, their stepfather and his two sons still live. They enjoy their freedom, feeling absolutely no remorse for the evil they perpetrated on these two children. Nor are they repentant for the emotional havoc each of them has foisted onto young minds and souls.

And still, the same kinds of vicious assaults are occurring today and tonight. Deena and Starla are aware that every day and every night some predator is stalking the young, the unprotected. And they also know that too many people, especially those in a position to know, will sit idly by, doing nothing, hiding their heads in the sand, pretending that nothing unusual is taking place.

Those uninvolved and uncaring people, many of them relatives, even mothers or fathers, would rather allow the viciousness to continue than face the fact there is evil in the family. Dirty family secrets are kept in the closet, or swept under the rug.

Perhaps those bystanders are afraid they will lose their husband, or their son, or their brother. Afraid what the 'neighbors would think', of the stigma if the truth were to be revealed. Afraid that the rest of their family would shun them, should they speak up.

Or it may be fear that they could be forced to live alone, without the companionship or support provided by the abuser.

Deena, especially emphatic, and Starla are committed to revealing what happens all too often when a sexual monster is in a position to take advantage of a youngster, a prey unable to defend herself or himself (oh yes, it happens to males, too; remember the Catholic priests recently in the news?), children without a champion within their family. Perhaps somewhere, in another family, Deena's story and Starla's story may give someone courage to act, to stop or prevent similar evil manipulations of their own young children. Not very likely, considering that such protective actions have been minimal in the past. But hopefully at least one person or one parent who reads these words will be moved to interfere, to say "No!"

These happenings will be related in a mélange of bits and pieces, fragmented, as the trauma of Deena and Starla's childhood memories surface, as the women try to relate the wicked events that their depraved stepfather and stepbrother executed on each of them.

But, it was not only the family who committed these vile acts. It was also friends and companions of the family as well as others—from bad to worse.

It is the author's intent to convey the emotions and the feelings, using as close to Deena and Starla's precise words as is possible, while bearing in mind the sensitivity of the subject and the reader.

There will be no attempt made to clean up the descriptions that emerged from the massive flow of tears and wails of anguish that came from these two tortured sisters. Each woman will speak as she remembers her individual ordeal. There was no joint interview, no attempt to join the two women's accounts of suffering together. It is mainly for that reason there will be instances where each one remembers the situation somewhat differently. That is understandable, because they were only young children, as the events began to unfold.

Events, as they are related, may be more or less in chronological order. However, minds so abused by the torment that both Deena and Starla suffered would not always follow a sequential pattern, so these events will be recorded as the women recall them and, as much as possible, in their own halting, agonizing, emotion-filled words.

This author apologizes in advance for the grammar and misuse of words and punctuation in the manuscript of which there will be many. Attempting to relate the troubling re-living of such a vile period of their lives, it is necessary to take substantial liberty with the standard grammar rules to try to place emphasis where it is needed. May my publisher, her editors and you, dear readers, forgive the lapses that will certainly occur throughout this book.

~ * ~

All reluctance aside, I feel very honored—in fact, more than honored. Although Deena has undergone analysis to enable her to cope with the havoc wreaked on her life, I am informed that this is the very first time that Starla has been willing to discuss the situation. Not just with a man, but with anyone. The severe trauma of the sexual abuse and misuse by a series of individuals including her stepfather and his sons, and many other friends that both the mother and the stepfather brought around, has had even more dire results in Starla's situation. The constant mistreatment, even after she approached young adulthood, has the result of causing her to turn away from society, and seek solace elsewhere.

Little wonder that there was a lot of drugs used to help alleviate the situation and to ease a tortured soul. Little wonder that with nothing but vile experiences with the male population, Starla chooses not to have any contact with men of any sort, turning instead to the female gender for solace. It is nothing short of bewilderment that she is willing to meet with me and to bare her anguished inner being to help describe the monsters that existed in her childhood. And those monsters continue to live today.

The trauma of sexual exploitation for an entire childhood and teen-age years affect different people in very different ways. Especially, two people with the diverse personalities of Deena and Starla. So, a quick word of explanation is needed here.

Deena has miraculously survived the massive flood of mental anguish that was heaped upon her and her sister. She has found some relief in her life and has focused her mind onto her son and her own self-improvement. Great strides have been made, yet there isn't a single minute that goes by without some recollection of the horror of a sexual predator stalking her day and night

Her ability to bring herself back to a normal life speaks volumes about the inner strength and intestinal fortitude that she possesses in huge quantities.

Starla, on the other hand, found a different way to cope with the outpouring of evil that threatened to drown her. She focused on her children to a large degree, and the disability of her older son was just one more blow she had to suffer. Turning to drugs in the search of some relief, Starla sought solace in her own fashion. The constant use of a wide variety of drugs, and the dominating memories of her childhood sexual violations have had everlasting effects.

Starla has turned away from relationships with men and seeks comfort with the less intrusive presence of female friends. Yes, she found lesbianism to be less threatening and more caring. There is, however, one male with whom Starla can't distance herself. That male is 'George.'

'George' is Starla's private, personal male demon that lives in her head. He just won't go away.

A victim of frequent overdoses of a variety of drugs, Starla's speech is slurred, her words difficult to understand. Lack of dental care during her childhood has caused several of her front teeth to deteriorate and they have been removed. 'George' has stolen her replacement teeth and has hidden them away. He does that quite often. Encouraged to obtain replacements, Starla says that 'George' will eventually bring her teeth back when he has finished with them. He always does.

'George' is often taking other things as well, hiding them and then bringing them back in his own time. 'George' even steals money from Starla and hides it. Most of the time, 'George' doesn't bring the money back, spending it on himself.

~ * ~

The stories of these two women will be told deliberately using first names only, in order to protect some of those who were innocently involved, and others involved only to a small degree. Unfortunately, this will also partially shield the guilty from public scrutiny. Be that as it may, the perpetrators, their friends, and their families will all know.

There will be no deliberate attempt by the author to unfairly place blame on anyone or to abase anyone. However, the details herein will be true and complete, as precise as the memory of a four-year-old infant and a five-year-old child can remember; unedited in any way. And there will be a minimum of profanity.

The events speak for themselves. If you really wanted to dig through the dirt, you may be able to identify the families involved, but that's on you. At times, this story will be graphic, but realize that the truth is not always soft, cozy, warm and comfortable. Reality is often hard.

It will be for you, the reader, to judge the actions of all of the people involved, especially the adults. You may determine the degree of shame, blame and guilt that each carries.

Let's get to know the two tortured women and hear of their horrendous childhood.

----DEENA----

Before Deena begins her story, let me present her to you, as she is now. Here is an attractive, thirty-five-year old woman, reasonably well adjusted, confident and determined to get on with her life. Reactivating a strong yen for learning that had been stunted by the viciousness of her childhood, she is an honor student at a local University, where she plans to achieve her degree fifty percent faster than the normal student. A leader in the student activities, she puts group accomplishments and aid for the disadvantaged students at the top of her goal chart.

She has a young son from an earlier marriage, and remains on a friendly basis with her ex-husband, Steve. She is aware of the need to keep both responsible parents involved in their child's life, and minimize the effects that a split family would have.

Putting as many of her past troubles behind her as possible, through therapy and self-motivation,

Deena plans on continuing to be a fine example to her neighbors, her friends, and her family. She faces the upcoming marriage with a lot of excitement, and a little fear, but with the knowledge that someone cares for her unconditionally, without restriction, without reservation.

----STARLA----

Starla has come through her life's difficulty a little differently than Deena. Becoming a mother of a male child at the age of fifteen, Starla is now the mother of two young men. The first child suffered diminished capacity, but Starla still devotes much of her life to her sons.

While not being the dedicated scholar type, Starla graduated from high school. In as much as there was no financial assistance coming from her family, Starla entered into the work force seeking to provide food and shelter for her family, as well as providing the security for her children that she had never experienced either as a child or as a young woman.

After suffering an abusive marriage that ended in divorce, Starla finds the companionship of women much less of a threat to her physical and mental well-being. She shuns the attention of any male, but still can't escape 'George.'

She would like to evict 'George' but he refuses to leave. He just stays and torments Starla, harassing her by hiding things from her.

Starla has grown accustomed to 'George' and speaks of him in a tolerant way. So far, he hasn't violated her and if he left, she would be completely alone.

Without delaying further, let's learn about the evils visited upon these valiant young women, two courageous persons who have survived such catastrophic childhoods: Deena and her sister Starla, victims of sexual perverts who prey on little baby girls and young boys.

My Sister and I/Owensby

Chapter 1

----Deena----

"Cliff's your daddy now!"

With these words, my mother brought demons of Hell into my childhood. She delivered me into the warped hands of a vicious child molester and his evil sons. My mother, by allowing this monster to move in with our family, destroyed my life and brought ruin to my older sister, Starla.

"Oh, God! If you are really there, how could you allow this to happen to your innocent young children? Where is your mercy? Your abundant merciful love? Why do you not strike these bastards dead?"

Why? Mother, why?

Step-daddy—no—I don't even want to use that phrase for him. Cliff was never a daddy, not of any kind. Daddies protect and nurture their children, even those obtained by marriage or by adoption. Daddies don't sexually abuse little girls, nor allow their evil sons to abuse little girls. Daddies don't give their little girls to strangers to use as sex toys.

No, Cliff, you were never a daddy. You were and always will be a monster—a fiend.

And what you did to my sister and me, what you allowed your sons, your friends and your acquaintances to do to us, arouses my fiercest emotions. Rage! Burning, flaming, molten hot, anger-fed hatred; may you burn in Hell forever!

And mother, you just stood by; ignoring, turning your back, and pretending you didn't know what Starla and I were going through.

Yeah.

Sure you didn't know.

~ * ~

Angry? Angry? Damn right, I'm angry! Jack, you would be fuming. You should be angry. Everyone should be angry. There should be a freaking lynch mob! I would be delighted to be the first to pull the noose tight on the necks of those bastards.

Perhaps I take after my mother. My first memory of my mother is of her anger. My mother was almost always angry. And she showed it—often.

In 1973, at the age of three, I had the occasion to see that rage in action. My mother had been employed as the manager of an apartment complex in Asheboro, North Carolina. Included with the job was a free apartment. I never knew what really happened, perhaps she lost her job or just fell out with the owner, but suddenly we were getting ready to move. And Mom wanted us kids to trash the apartment.

That's right! Trash it. Really trash it—stuff garbage and things down the drain, and in the toilet. My sister took my diaper, still filled with baby shit, and smeared it on the walls. That really caused an impression on my young mind, as I was always told, "No, no" regarding my diaper and the mess it held. Now, it was okay to rub it everywhere.

We ripped holes in the carpet, knocked holes in the walls, and lit matches on the floor. Really trashed everything. Then we moved far away. To a town called Ramseur.

Actually, it was only a distance of about twelve miles, but to a three-year old, that's a long, long way. Into a small house, my mother, me, my two older sisters and my two older brothers all moved in.

Let's get one thing straight early on. I am telling this in the manner of how a thirty-five year old woman remembers the times and the events when she was just barely four-years old. There is just no way that I can completely recapture the feelings, the horror, and the terror that I experienced, or that any child would suffer. If I could, you probably couldn't believe it, or else, it might just make you sick. I can only relate as best I can the way I remember what and how I felt when I was a child, and the things that happened to me.

But that comes up way short of what my true feelings were at the time. I don't have the words to describe to them and I doubt if we could put down on paper—the paper would catch fire—the sensations, the lost feelings, the disappointments, the heartbreak that a violated child goes through. Nor the shame or lonely, deserted, desolate feeling that a child feels when she or he has been convinced that she or he is worthless.

There is no adult who can comprehend the depth of complete despair that a child has when there is no one to reach out to. No father, no mother, no one.

I only have one early childhood memory of my father, and that involved anger as well. Daddy came to the house where we had moved. I remember that he had a shirt pocket full of cigars, and that he was on his knees, crying, begging my mother to take him back. My mother began cursing him, swearing at him, throwing things at him, trying to beat on him.

Finally, she went to a closet and took out a baseball bat, threatening to kill him if he didn't leave. I don't actually remember him leaving, but I suppose that he did. At least, she didn't kill him.

There was an aftermath.

Several days later, someone broke into our house. My grandmother raised Penny. I don't remember if Penny was my mother's half sister, or if she was adopted, or if my grandmother just took her in. At any rate, the people who broke into our house were after Penny. Well, it wasn't exactly a break in, but a man, dressed in a police uniform of some kind, knocked on the front door, and one of us kids opened the door and let him in. A woman stepped in behind the man, and I remember that she had a cow chain. My mother was in the hallway. When she saw the woman, she screamed for us kids to run and hide. Penny ran into the closet to hide, and when my sister tried to run into the closet, Penny pushed her away and wouldn't let my sister hide in the closet with her.

The house was very small, and we kids all slept in one bedroom. I remember us running into the bedroom and trying to crawl under the bed. The woman came into the room and kept trying to drag us from under the bed, pinching and twisting our feet and legs. We kicked and fought and screamed and cried. Finally, all of the kids jumped out the window and ran into the woods. The woman hit my mother in the face with the chain, breaking her nose. Both the man and the woman beat up my mother rather badly. They beat on my mother with both the cow chain and a bottle they had picked up.

    I don't remember exactly how or when they left, but when the two invaders had left, we kids returned to the house. Sometime later, I remember being in Cliff's car. He had somehow gotten an old Cadillac and some of us were in the car with him when the two people who had broken into our house began chasing us down the road. They were shooting at us. My sister screamed for me to get down, get on the floor. And I did. I remember hearing a lot of gunshots, and I saw Cliff reaching for his shotgun. He stopped the car and then jumped out with the gun. They argued, Cliff and the other people, back and forth for a while. That man and that woman, the same ones that broke into our house, were in that other car. They argued a lot.

Cliff was holding the shotgun, which he pointed at the car behind us. He told them that if they didn't leave he was going to blow their heads off. I guess they believed him because, eventually, they left.

About two weeks later, the police came to the house and told my mother that someone had called in and said there was a bomb in the house. We kids were allowed to sit in the police car while the officers searched the house. They found something taped to the bottom side of the toilet lid, but I never learned what it was. At any rate, it didn't explode and we were finally allowed to go back inside. My mother sent us all straight to bed, but she didn't join us. At least, she didn't, not at that time.

During these early years, it seemed that there was always a man around, but not always the same man. Perhaps my mother was lonely, or perhaps she just had to have a male companion. One of these was a man by the name of Toby. Toby was into music, and always wanted the kids to dance for him in the living room. Living room, front room, great room, it was all the same. The house was small, and there were not many rooms.

As far as Toby went, there just seemed to be something strange and weird about him. Something strange that even at the age of three and four that I just couldn't like. With four older children in my family, it's not likely that I was just being shy, but there was something there that just turned me away from Toby.

And then Cliff began to come around all of the time. It wasn't long until he bedded down my mother, if he hadn't already. He was around a lot. Cliff and his monster of a son: Michael. And the Demons of Hell were about to open wide their gaping jaws and suck me and Starla inside.

---Starla---

Yeah, I remember trashing the apartment. I must have been about five. I am the middle child, with one sister and one brother older than I was at that time. I also had a younger sister, Deena. There were four children and later a brother was born. That made me the middle child.

I don't believe that my memory will be as clear as Deena's on much of our childhood. There was just too much that happened, too many bad things and bad people. Since then, I have used too many drugs and smoked too much pot; took too many pills; and snorted too much stuff. Good stuff and bad stuff. I used it all.

I try hard to remember some of the good times that we had as children, some of the joy. But I can't. Isn't that funny? I can't remember a single time that we laughed or played in fun or had a good time. It was always bad, always fighting, always beating.

I remember that my momma was the manager of the apartment building where we were living. Part of her agreement with the owner was that she would manage the apartments, collect the rent and keep the areas clean. That's what she made us kids do, clean everything and wash everything. If it wasn't clean, we would get a beating and then have to clean it again. If it still wasn't clean enough to satisfy her, we would get another beating. There was always a beating—every day. Sometimes she would just beat us in case there was anything that we had done wrong that she didn't know about. I guess you could call that her 'just in case beating.'

I can't say that my momma was sleeping with the owner of the apartment building. However, knowing her morals, I would bet that she was. And not only with him.

And it must have been because she either refused him or because she began seeing another man, Cliff, that caused the manager to fire her and he gave us a week to leave.

Of course, she gave us orders to trash the place. What did you expect? She was an evil woman. Only Deena was too little to do much, but the older kids took the diapers full of baby shit and spread it in the carpet and on the walls. We tore up the carpet, threw stuff around, knocked holes in the walls, and tore up the cabinets, then put canned food down the sink in the bathroom. And we did a lot of other damage.

And then we moved into the white house in Ramseur with the little building out in back, which would become our club. And that was where all the sexual shit started happening.

My momma was working in a restaurant in Asheboro and at that time she was single. She was screwing around with the owner of the white house in order to pay the rent. I remember him trying to mess with me one time, but nothing happened that I could remember. In fact, I think that he was the only one that didn't get me.

I remember that one time there was a horse. I don't know where the horse came from, or who owned it. I don't even know why I remember it. I do recall my oldest brother, Dean, being on the horse, and I remember hitting the horse on its butt. I don't know why I did it, but the horse took off with Dean on its back. Dean fell off, and then said that he was going to get me for that. I don't remember if he got me, but I'm pretty sure that he did. Most everyone got me. I don't know where the horse went.

We would all go and use the bathroom at night. We had to save water to keep the water bill as low as possible, so we all used the bathroom before it was flushed. Dean, the oldest, would be the last one to go and would flush the commode.

One night, just before Dean went into the bathroom, the police showed up. There was a bomb that had been attached to the commode. I remember the police saying that had we flushed the commode, the house would have blown up. I remember the police officer placing me in his car.

After that, my daddy took me home with him for a while. He was living in Cole Ridge, near my grandmother, but he had his own house. He was married to a woman by the name of Diane, which is the same name as my momma. I couldn't understand that.

We had gone to his house several times to spend some time with him. One time, while we were there, the movie *King Kong* was on TV. My brother, Chris, and I were laying on the floor (we all slept on the floor when we were there, all of the time), or perhaps, in the same bed. I remember lying in the doorway while trying to watch *King Kong*. It was not only my dad and his wife that were there, but there was another woman, as well. I don't remember who she was; I can't recall her name.

She saw Chris and me lying on the floor, watching the movie. She said, "All right, y'all come in here and watch the television."

So, Chris and I went into the room and got onto the couch. Chris was at one end and I was at the other. We watched the movie.

The next day, that woman had told my daddy that I had put my hand down my brother's pants and was playing with his penis.

They took me to an armchair and strapped me down. They, my stepmother—only I didn't call her that because she wasn't—and my daddy and the woman, strapped me to that chair. They kept accusing me of playing with Chris's penis. I kept saying no, I didn't do it.

They beat the hell out of me. All three of them beat me. They took turns, beating me with a belt. First it was my daddy and then his wife and then the other woman—over and over and over. It went on for a long time and it hurt. A lot. They were screaming at me for being a pervert. I could only cry and say that I hadn't done anything. And the beating went on.

Chris was so scared that he couldn't tell the truth. He told them that I did it, but only because they pressured him to the point that he lied.

I had a hard time with getting over that. Now, of course, I know that we were just kids and that there was nothing that any of us could have done about it.

Chris was always getting me into trouble.

This was the only time in my life that I can remember my momma taking up for me, but I think it was just for the money. I had been beaten pretty badly. I had bruises and cuts and marks and stuff. My momma came and picked me up. She took me to the hospital where they x-rayed me and stuff. I didn't have any broken bones, just bruises and whelps.

I never went back there again, never saw my daddy again except in court about it. And the court....the court wasn't for what he had done to me, it was about child support. My momma carried me with her. I was the only child that she took. And that was the last time I saw my daddy while I was a child. There, in court. There was a time later in my life, but that's a different story. Maybe later.

There weren't really any good times in my life, only when I was at my Grandma's. I don't remember any good times with my momma. Not a single one. Not one damn time.

Chapter 2

---Deena---

Can you imagine yourself being a four-year-old infant sitting naked on a kitchen countertop with a man's sticky, gooey semen all over your face, your body, and on your hands and in your hair? How about in your mouth? Ugh!

Does hearing about that disgust you? If so, you're going to have a real problem with the rest of my story. If you're reading this in a book and you're turned off now, you had better not read the rest, it only gets worse.

But, then, so did my life.

"Don't tell anyone!" Cliff commanded.

As a four year old, what are you going to do? Sitting there confused, terrified, facing an adult who had just forced me to have oral sex with him, ejaculating into my mouth, at an age when I didn't even know what oral sex was. And I didn't dare to get sick or spit out the salty, warm liquid he shot into my mouth and throat.

"Just don't tell anyone. Go take a bath and clean up this stuff." His strange, hard glare was scary.

Orders from adults were to be obeyed. My mother had taught me that, the hard way. When she told one of the kids to do something, brutal, even severe beatings, now politely called 'Corporal Punishment', followed immediately unless we jumped into action. Even at my age. And since Cliff was an adult, I had to do as I was told. So, I took towels and mopped up the juice he had shot off all over the cabinets and over me, and then washed myself.

Yeah. Sure. Don't tell anyone. Hide the dirty deed. At the time, I was scared—shocked and confused. It didn't seem just right, but Cliff told me that was what I was made for, what all females were made for, and just for that.

I can see the sickness of it all now, but at the time, I only knew that I was supposed to obey any order given to me by an adult. And not tell anyone. Or else, get the hell beat out of me.

What Cliff was doing there in the house remains a mystery to me even today. For some reason, he was keeping me. I was only four years old, so my memory is only partially clear. My mother was not in the house. I'm not sure if she was working, or even if she had a job, only that she wasn't there. I don't even know where she was, and I've never been able to ask her.

At any rate, Cliff was staying with me. Outside behind the house was a small sand pile where I often played. Somehow, I had come up with a straw and was sticking it in the sand and trying to drink the sand. Who knows why a four-year old child would to that, perhaps I thought it was a milkshake or something. Whatever the idea, Cliff caught me doing that and made me go into the house.

When I went inside, he picked me up and put me on the kitchen counter top and began brushing the sand off my face, out of my throat and the front of me. At that time, I don't know if it was unusual or what but I never wore a shirt or blouse. He just started rubbing all over me, telling me how pretty I was. It's amazing that you can remember all these things, but that was the point where I really got scared. I think that's why I remember it so clearly, because I got really, really scared.

He continued to rub my body and then began rubbing himself. I didn't know what he was doing; I didn't understand what was going on. Then, he pulled his pants down and basically forced my head onto him, forcing his hard penis into my mouth, almost choking me and holding onto me until he was finished. When he got finished, he told me to stop crying, to clean up, that I would get used to it; that's what little girls are for, that's what women are for. And good for nothing else.

Tell you what happened, Jack? Don't you understand? He continued rubbing my body and made me rub his. Yes, even his balls. He made me hold his penis in my hands and showed me how to rub him and then he made me put the thing in my mouth and suck on it. After a few minutes, you can guess what happened.

Scared at the sudden flow of salty, nasty fluids that I tried to spit out and that ran down my face and neck; I was crying, knowing that something was wrong. Cliff told me to quit crying, there was nothing wrong. That I would get used to it. That this was what all little girls are for and that's what women were made for and this is what my mother did for him. And that this was what I was going to do for him. And these are the same things he told me my whole life.

And, I remember being scared when I first saw his body because I didn't......I knew what my brothers' bodies looked like; because we grew up like, you know, stair-steps. We were fairly close in age, my brothers and sisters, but I'd never seen a grown man's body before...you know...all hairy and all.

What did I think? I was scared, I. .... I don't really remember what I thought, I just remember being confused and not knowing what to do, and he undressed me, putting his hands all over my body, and putting my hands on his body, and then showing me how he wanted me to move my hands.

After I was cleaned up, he repeated his instructions that I should not tell anyone, and that if I told my mother that she would just get mad and beat me again. As I often received this kind of punishment, I believed him, and naturally, didn't tell anyone. Especially my mother.

Something that I have just this moment realized. It is extremely hard for me to identify my mother as 'Mom' or 'Mommy,' which signifies a certain amount of tenderness and love, and I'm not sure that I ever saw even the slightest sign of that from my mother. Since she was my mother is a biological fact, I will refer to her as mother. Not Mother, just mother.

She was twenty-five when I was born, and she had my younger brother, who was born after Cliff and my mother were married, and so there were six of us children. And there had been two miscarriages.

Guess you could say that she really knew how to get pregnant. But from the way she treated all of us kids, it was easy to see that she didn't have those babies because she loved babies.

Of course, Cliff wasn't lacking in that department either. In fact, with his first wife, he had fathered five kids before he began to shack up with my mother. Two of them, Michael and Robert turned out to be younger versions of Cliff. Michael was eleven or twelve years older than me, and Robert a year or so older than Michael.

Cliff hadn't moved in with us yet. I remember his children coming over and there was a clubhouse— well, we called it a clubhouse. It was just this old shack that was behind the house that we were in, and we were trying to fix it up to be our clubhouse. We had bricks propping the curtains up. We were just kids. We didn't realize that they would fall on us. I went to move the curtains and a part of one of the bricks fell and hit me on the head and made me bleed.

For some reason, Cliff was the one who came to pick me up. I was bleeding pretty badly. Cliff took me to his trailer and washed my head. He put me into the bathtub. I was crying and upset, had a big goose egg on my head, you know. It was, like, on the crown of my head. And I was in the bathtub. He decided to join me in the bathtub. It was the same old thing, you know, just made me give him oral sex. I guess he thought it was cleaner in the bathtub, but I remember my head hurting so badly. Sorry. I know it's crude—it is *very* crude. But I remember because he had his hands on my head and I remember my head hurting so badly and he kept putting his fingers where the brick had hit me, and it hurt more when he did that.

And then he got me out of the bathtub, when he had finished, and cleaned me up and everything. I remember sitting on the steps of the trailer, and I was crying. I was still crying when my mother got there, and I guess she put it off as pain from where the brick had hit me. But, that had been hours before, you know, and I guess that I'm pissed off at her that she didn't really notice. The brick had hit me hours before, and I'm still crying. And she didn't even frigging notice! Don't you think she should have seen? That she should have known something worse was wrong with me?

Cliff's children would come over and visit. We finally got that clubhouse cleaned out, and we would sit in there and tell ghost stories, or whatever. Michael always used to sit beside me. We would take turns telling ghost stories. Michael told me that he wanted to show me something. Someone said that it was my sister's turn to tell a ghost story. When she tried to talk, she couldn't say anything clearly. It sounded like her mouth was full. The lights were out, it was night and dark outside, and there were no lights in the clubhouse. There we were, in the dark, telling ghost stories.

Michael said that he wanted me to see something, and when my sister tried to speak with her mouth full, Michael turned on his flashlight. His brother, Robert, had his penis stuck in my sister's mouth. I was horrified and scared. Although I was younger, I knew exactly what she was feeling, what she was dealing with, but I was too little to do anything.

It never stops. It just never stops.

---Starla---

It seemed like there was always arguments between my momma and my daddy. There was never a home life.

There was a sheriff down there named Dean. I always thought it was strange that both of my brothers were named Joe. One was named Joe Dean. And I found out later that my daddy claimed that one of us kids was not his, one of us was the child of my mother and the sheriff.

I used to think that I was the one that wasn't my daddy's, because I'm short, with very short legs, and the rest of the family are tall with long legs. But then, my mother would always slap me around when I was little and tell me that I was exactly like my daddy.

When we were living in the white house, before Cliff and his family moved in, things weren't too bad. Our mother was working and we kids got along. There was just our mother and the five of us kids. Still, there were frequent beatings when our mother came home in a bad mood, which was almost every single night.

We walked to school. I started school at the same time that my older sister, Angie, did. We were both in kindergarten, as there was only eleven months difference in our ages.

No, that's not right. We didn't go to kindergarten, but our mother enrolled us both in school at the same time. I probably should have waited a year before going to school, but my mother worked and needed for me to be in school. So she enrolled me at the same time that Angie started.

Afterwards, the school authorities held me back for an additional year in the first grade, while Angie was promoted. I did real good, receiving grades of As and Bs, but they said that I wasn't mature enough to go on, so they held me back, which made me hate school. That made Angie one grade ahead of me.

Every once in a while I would do some really stupid things.

We were walking to school along the road one day, and I put my toboggan over my face and head. I told Angie to watch me and make sure that I didn't go out into traffic, because we lived on the highway where there were a lot of cars.

The next thing I know, the teacher who was going down the same road, grabbed me. She put me into her car and took me to school. She called my momma. She said that I had walked out into traffic because I had a toboggan over my head.

That afternoon....of course, my sister got into trouble because she was older than I and was supposed to watch out for me. So, I got a beating, which I deserved. But so did Angie. She got a beating also and that really made me feel bad. I had thought it funny before, even when I was getting beat, but after Angie got her beating, it wasn't funny any more.

And Angie was always the one for me. Do you understand what I'm trying to say? I followed her around like a little puppy dog. Trying to be like my older sister, trying to copy her, trying to always be with her. Later on, I started following along after my brothers, but at this time Angie was always the one that I hung around with.

And, as I had short legs, I used to try to keep up with her. I'd run while she walked. At school one day I tried to keep up with her, because she was all I had, you know. And Angie hated it because I was always around, everywhere. You know, the younger sister.

Anyhow, at the school one day...Angie was one grade higher than I was and I was one grade lower than her.. But, I tried to keep up with her, because she was all I had, you know. And Angie haed it because I was always around, everywhere. You know, the younger sister. Anyhow, Angie got mad at me and went into the bathroom. Well, I followed her into there. When I did, she closed the door. Hard—broke my nose. And Angie....you know, I still followed Angie around.

There was a girl one time....I guess I was a violent person at that time, because I was always after Angie. But she wanted to be by herself in school. She was always trying to chase the little sister away, but I really did admire and love her, and I just wanted to be close to her.

Anyway, there was this girl that hung around with Angie a little bit when we were at school. At the front of the school there were these big columns, you know? And there were these steps leading up to the front entrance, perhaps five or ten steps, all very steep. Well, a girl was standing close to Angie. That was *my* place, I felt, and I wanted to be standing there, so I just pushed her. Hard. She fell down the steps. I thought that I had killed her. But, she got up.

Of course, Angie raised cane at me, because I had pushed her friend down the steps. But I just had to push her, didn't I? Because she took my sister away from me? I couldn't allow that, could I?

When I got older, I was the 'dryer.' That is, I hung out the clothes to dry. You know, on the clothesline. I used to say that I was the dryer and everybody would just laugh at me. Anyway, one day I was just standing out there. I was hanging out clothes when I felt something wet fall on my hand. I looked up, but there wasn't a bird or anything. When I looked at my hand, I saw that a drop of blood had fallen on me. I thought that it was something from God, like a sign of some kind. I still don't know where it came from.

It wasn't much longer before Cliff came into my life. Everything had been going along just okay, I guess. Then *he* came around—Cliff and his sons. He moved in and started telling us how he was going to take care of us. We had oatmeal for breakfast and beans for dinner—every single freaking day. With momma working, Cliff fixed breakfast every day. That's about the only effort he made to take care of any of us.

When Cliff moved in so did his two sons, Michael and Robert. Robert was about sixteen and Michael was about a year younger. And that's when the sexual shit really started.

At first, Robert would just take me out into the field and beat me. There were no sexual things, just the beating. He said that if I told anyone, it would be worse. I believed him, but I didn't know just how much worse it would get.

That old shack out behind our house was our clubhouse. We would sit on the floor of our clubhouse and talk, telling each other stories. At night, it would be very dark and we would tell ghost stories.

One night, Robert grabbed my head and forced my mouth open. I felt him put something warm and hard in my mouth and into my throat. It almost choked me, but Robert slapped me upside my head, and made me close my lips. He said that if I bit, he would kill me. I didn't know what it was.

It became my turn to tell a ghost story and I tried to tell the others that I didn't have a ghost story to tell. But I couldn't talk. My mouth was full of something and I couldn't speak. Someone turned on a light, and I could see Robert's stomach pressed against my face, his penis was in my mouth. About that time, my mouth filled up with something wet and salty. I couldn't spit it out, because Robert's penis was still in my mouth. Swallowing it almost made me throw up, but Robert just hit me again.

I had just turned six years old. Happy birthday, Starla!

Chapter 3

---Deena---

Before they moved into our house, Cliff's boys would come over and walk around completely naked. I can even tell you which of his children was circumcised and which one wasn't. Isn't that an awful thing for a little girl to know?

But, I guess from my reaction, that Michael decided that I was the one he was going to single out—his personal prey. I always thought that something must have happened to those boys for them to be that way, but I don't know if it's genetic or what or just. . .

Sorry, I get a little soggy sometimes.

Cliff lived in a trailer in Franklinville, North Carolina. Guess what else was there? A junkyard.

Franklinville was just one great big, huge junkyard. Cars everywhere, junk cars as far as you could see, and trailers. I don't know if Cliff's children were related to the owners in any way, or if it was just a convenient place to play. We played there all the time.

You know about red clay, how it's just a lot of red dust when it's dry? I was sitting on the tailgate of a truck, putting my foot down, you know into the dusty red mud, or in the dust, making footprints. I remember it being really, really hot.

Michael always found me in the junkyard. You know, a junkyard is a really good place to hide. But he found me and made me get into the front seat of the truck with him. That was the first time that I had ever been penetrated. He was about sixteen or seventeen and I was maybe six. It hurt—a lot. But Michael just laughed. He told me that it was supposed to hurt. That was part of being a woman, part of growing up, but that eventually I would get used to it. But by that time, I guess you could say that I was an old hand. You know what I mean? I knew what to expect from him. I knew what to expect from his dad, and I knew what his brother was doing to my sister.

Yeah, I knew. The first time with Michael, the first time that I can remember, was that for some reason I was spending the night with Michael's mother, in her trailer. Cliff wasn't living with her at that time. I guess she had already chased him off. She put me to bed, and she was good to me. That's the number one thing I remember about her; she was always good to all of us kids. She went out of the way to treat us like her own children. She was always good to her kids, and I was always jealous of them because they had a loving mother and they had it better than we did.

But, anyway, I was asleep in her daughter's bedroom. I don't remember if the daughter was there or not, but I do remember that I was the only one in the bedroom at the time. And Michael..... When I woke up, Michael had his knees on my shoulders making them hurt, and his penis in my face. I remember trying to fake like I was asleep, you know, but he forcefully opened my mouth and stuck that thing inside, making me gag. That was the first time with Michael.

And you know, the same damn things, the threats, the 'don't tell,' you know. I wanted to tell his mom so bad, but I was afraid. I just kept thinking that I was going to choke to death.

Why in God's name can that happen and no one hear it? I mean, that was in the seventies and trailers were cheap then. They're cheaply made now, but back then, the walls were all paper-thin. And nobody heard me choking?

Other times? Of course, there were other times. It seemed like it was *all* of the time. And there were other people after me, too. One of those was Raymond.

My mother had a friend, Becky, who was a babysitter for us kids. There was an outhouse behind the house we were staying in. Although it wasn't being used any longer, it still stood on the property. Raymond was a teenager, at least old enough to drive. I was still five or six years old. He took me into the outhouse and made me give him oral sex. He was just like the others.

Tell someone? Who could I tell? Everyone knew. Or should have known. At least it seemed to me that everyone knew. That didn't leave anyone else to tell. I couldn't tell Becky, because she was good to us kids, much better and much kinder than our own mother. Now, I realize that I must have known what Raymond was doing was wrong, but if I had told Becky, that would destroy her family. And my mother would just have beaten me again.

Who the hell was I going to tell?

My mother had a brother, Mike. I was staying with my grandmother at the time, whether for several days or for the night, I don't remember. He got to drinking, and became tanked. It was the same thing, all hands, rubbing and stroking. Then he broke down crying, sobbing. I would tell him that it was okay, that he shouldn't cry. I'd tell him that just so he would go away.

Michael's mother had remarried. I always thought that if I told that man about Cliff, he would kill Cliff, but I was always afraid. Much too frightened to tell anyone about Cliff. And, I had come to realize that Cliff meant something to my family.

We were poor. No, not just poor, but really, *really* poor—trailer trash poor. I don't know if my mother made any money, but she never seemed to have any. I know it's weird, but we were poor, even to eating the same pot of beans for a week. Oatmeal for breakfast and beans for dinner. And that was it—for days and days. And, when Cliff would come around, there was more money for food, more money for clothes, you know. There was.... And I knew that if I ran him off, everybody would hate me. Everybody would hate me, because there wouldn't be that much food. And I don't know if you've ever been hungry, but....... We were hungry. And, uh, we were the 'white trash', you know, we were the kids that the other kids' parents wouldn't let their children play with.

Well, I started elementary school. At that time, you took a nickel to school for milk. Yeah, back in the mid 1970s for five cents you could get milk at school. I never had five cents. I just had to watch all the other children drinking milk and eating their snacks. We were so poor that I never had a nickel; we just couldn't even raise five cents for me.

After a while, I guess that my school homeroom teacher noticed. Evidently she told someone at the church that she went to about us, and one day some of the church members showed up at our house with bags of food. My mother was very pleasant while the visitors were there. But the moment they left, she got really pissed off, swearing and threatening to beat the kid that told those people how poor we were half to death. I was scared and I lied, although I knew it was my teacher that had done this.

Thinking back, I think perhaps that the fact that I was only going to school for half a day, every day, gave my mother the false sense of security in that I didn't need to eat a snack or have milk. The other children were going for a full day, and would each eat lunch and have milk. I suppose that my mother just assumed that I would not have to eat at the school. Not that there was much to eat when I got home. It wasn't long after that until I was getting milk at school. I am certain that it was my teacher who was paying for it. God bless her.

I also knew that if Cliff left, there would never be money for milk, or for anything else, and that the other kids would be hungry again. Or, perhaps, I should say more hungry because it seemed that we were always hungry, never having enough. I also knew that if I told my mother what Cliff, Michael and Robert were doing to me and to my sister, that she would chase Cliff off, and we would only have oatmeal and beans again. So, I didn't dare tell her. Although, today, I am one hundred percent certain that she was aware of what was going on, but was so afraid of losing Cliff that she pretended not to know. Some loving mother! No wonder I was jealous of Cliff's children's mother's love.

---Starla---

Soon, it wasn't only Robert who was making me suck his penis; it was also Michael and Cliff. And it happened often, almost every day. At least one of them would be after me, promising me that if I behaved like a good girl they would leave my sisters alone. And I believed them.

It wasn't long until Robert would be taking me into the field to beat me. Then he would make me pull off my panties and lay on the ground. He would lie on top of me and put his penis in me. At first there was a lot of pain, but eventually I became used to it. He would soil me, spewing his semen on me and then just get up and leave me lying there as if nothing happened.

I guess he told his brother and his father, and it wasn't long before the two of them were doing the same thing. By the time I was seven it was an almost every day occurrence. They would tell me that was why I had been born, why every girl had been born, to please a man. And it was my duty to serve the men.

Cliff also threatened to do the same to my sisters if I misbehaved, and he also threatened to leave us if I didn't let him do his thing to me. He said that we wouldn't have a father, or a mother, and that we wouldn't have any money. He said the Welfare People would take us and put us in strange homes. I couldn't let that happen to my sisters or my brothers so I kept my mouth shut and just let them do what they wanted.

They told me that I would get to where I liked it, but they lied. That never happened. It was always just one more chore to do.

You want to know how messed up those boys were? I couldn't have been more than seven years old when Michael would make me stand over him while he was lying on his back and pee on him. That's right; urinate on his body. Ain't that just sick?

I didn't know what was going on. I was just a little girl. And every chance they got, they would stick it in me—over and over and over. And not just them, but others, as well.

There was a baby sitter that stayed with us for a while. He was just as bad as Cliff, Robert and Michael. He wanted to stick it in me and it didn't matter to him where. He would use my mouth and then my vagina. It disgusted me, and I was beginning to hate all adult men.

My momma was working and would leave me with my grandmother. I was asleep in one of the beds when my grandfather came into the room and began messing with me; touching and feeling and probing. He tried to get into bed with me but I got up and went into my grandmother's room—they didn't sleep together at the time—and got into bed with her. He left me pretty much alone after that. Still, I tried not to get too close to him. It got to where I would just wait until my momma came home. She would get there about ten-thirty, so I would stay up until she came, and then I would sleep with her.

It was while I was at my grandmother's house that I got scared. There was something happening with the baby-sitter and me, and there was something strange coming out of me. It was a smelly, yellow liquid that was oozing out of my vagina. I didn't know what it was, but it scared me to death. It messed up my shorts, really making them stink. I was too frightened to tell my grandmother about it, so I would take my shorts and wash them by hand, trying to get the yellow stain out.

    The baby-sitter was a grown man. Raymond.

    Oh, God! Won't it ever stop?

Chapter 4

---Deena---

One problem that I have had since birth is an immature bladder. In plain language, that means that my bladder is much smaller than normal, and that I must urinate more often than most people. In fact, if I don't visit the bathroom often, even now as an adult, I will have a problem. And you may well imagine the situation I was in as a child. Bedwetting was the norm for me, despite every attempt by my mother to make me stop. And it developed that the immature bladder became a problem at school as well.

At the kindergarten-or rather, at the school, there were set times when you would be allowed to use the bathroom, but only those set hours. That was okay for the people with normal bladders, but my immature bladder would fill up rather quickly, and I often wet myself, as I could not disrupt the class by being allowed to use the bathroom out of turn.

There was a box at the schoolhouse where parents would donate clothes that were no longer of use to their own children, and I would frequently arrive home, wearing clothes different from the ones that I had worn to the school. I carried my wet clothes along in a sack.

Let me set the scene for you. Our house was road-side to US Highway 64, a very busy, heavily traveled road. A lot of traffic would pass in front of our house. When I would arrive home with my wet clothes, my mother would make me put my wet pants over my head and stand outside on the front porch, often for hours. Can you, in your wildest imagination, believe that any mother would treat her own child in such a manner? Make a six-year-old girl stand out on the front porch with 'pissy pants' over her head, while everybody in the world went by? Would you do it?

I just don't understand. You can't shame a child into stopping something they can't control.

They did try to make my bladder grow, even though my mother didn't know that I had an immature bladder at that time. She would put beer in my milk bottle, hoping that would help me control its actions. Beer for a baby! Can you believe that?

My mother didn't really want children. She didn't need kids, I think. My grandmother, my mother's mother, was a preacher—a virtual zealot or fanatic. And I know that now a lot of religions look down on that. If you were to ask my other sisters about my grandmother, you'll find that they put her on a pedestal. To them, she was the end-all, be-all. But to me. . . . Well, she played favorites, my grandmother did. My older sister was certainly her favorite. But I think my mother was rebelling against my grandmother, and never turned back.

My mother's father was a terrible alcoholic. I barely remember him interacting with us. I just remember him being there, because we would walk from the school through the woods to my grandmother's house after we got out of school, sometimes. But I think she worked second shift, so it was only occasionally we were able to walk to grandma's house. And I remember my grandfather being there, working on a lawn mower. He was always working on a lawn mower, you know, and drinking!

I remember that alcohol was not allowed in grandmother's house, and she made my grandfather keep his refrigerator, where he kept his beer, under the carport. That was the only place where he could have beer.

You know, it was kind of strange. I guess her religion was called Holiness or something like that. But, you know, she would speak in tongues and that's how they. . .

You know, I look at it now, and you know, even though I grew up in it and it was normal for me at the time, I look at it now and to go and sit in a service like that would scare the hell out of me. Just... My relationship with God now is so different; I just don't see how that sort of fanaticism (because that's exactly what it is to me) can be healthy.

I don't think that...... And they call it, you know, being filled with the Ghost, and that....that's wonderful for them, but I don't..... and it would scare me and I don't want to expose my child to it.

They believe that.....

And, that's another thing. You see this; this two-inch scar here on my wrist? When I was a little girl, I was running through the woods behind my grandmother's house and I tripped over some fencing, I mean like it was really thick woods back there. Well, evidently, my dumb-ass pawpaw had been throwing his beer bottles in one particular place, and over the years there was a pile of broken bottles and glass. I never knew it was there. We were playing. . .gosh. . .we were playing hide and seek, or something. There was a piece of chicken coop that had been thrown over this pile of glass and my foot got caught in a piece of wire, and I fell. I put my hand down; falling onto a piece of glass and it cut my wrist. A pretty severe cut. They never took me to the doctor. Never gave it a thought. They took me into the house, and prayed over me.

Okay. Now look at the size of this scar. And think about it. The size of this cut on a five-year-old child's wrist. I damn near cut my hand off and these stupid people were praying over me, sprinkling olive oil over my head. But some verse in the Bible, I don't know exactly where, something about stopping the flow of blood, or whatever. Well, the whole church came over, you know, and they were all praying over me.

Alright.

Well, you know what? The entire time they were praying over me they've got this thing wrapped around my hand soaking up the blood. Eventually, blood flow will stop, or you will die. You know, that's really the only two choices. And then when the bleeding stopped, it was a miracle! It was a miracle that I didn't die, okay? I mean....but they were convinced that they had prayed me healthy. They were convinced of that.

I don't know how in the hell I ever lived. I really don't know how I lived. I don't know how any of us lived. I do know that there's not one of us kids who came out of the situation that we grew up in, who is completely emotionally stable. I..er...I sometimes think that perhaps I come the closest, but there's still times in my life that I. . .If I give in to it, it will stop me. Because I'm. . .well, you know me, Jack. Look at the anger that I carry. And, you know, that sometimes when people meet me, and they don't know me that well, and I get angry over something, to them it's just a ridiculous amount of anger. I know where it's coming from, but I doubt. . .and people talk about Anger Management. Well, that's just a bunch of B.S. I'm sorry, but I just don't agree with it. I'm angry, and I'm going to be angry probably until the day I die. And that's just the way it is. It's something that I have to put up with. You can't be forced to have sex from the time you're four years old and not grow up a little bit pissed off.

---Starla---

Raymond was a baby sitter that my momma paid to take care of us kids, especially Deena and me. He was a grown man and I believe that he was aready married. Raymond would come to my granny's house and pick me up and then take me out into one of the fields where he would make me take off my shorts and then lie down on the ground. He would stick his penis in me and ejaculate while licking my face. It hurt, but he didn't care, he just stood up and put the ugly thing back in his pants and would walk away, leaving me to get along the best I could. For a seven-year-old child, that wasn't any too good.

What the hell is it about grown men? It was bad enough that Robert was in his teens and so was Michael. Eventually, Robert quit messing with me, but it wasn't until he got married that he stopped.

Michael just kept on and so did Cliff. Why can't grown men leave little children alone?

It's not like we knew anything about sex. And it wasn't like it felt good, cause it never did. At least, not to me—it hurt every time. Every damn time! And it was dirty. I always had something sticky on me—some sticky shit—and there would be the dirt, but they didn't care.

My momma would leave me with Raymond and his wife. I don't know if she knew what was going on or not, but the yellow stuff just kept coming out of my vagina. Raymond and his wife had a son and a daughter. They picked up on the fact that I was losing liquid from my vagina. The son thought that it might be my 'woman's period' beginning, at the age of seven or seven and a half, but the daughter told him it was too early. Never did find out what was causing it.

One day, Cliff had me in the bed with my clothes off. He had his penis stuck in me and was pounding away when my older sister Angie walked in. She didn't say anything, but Cliff stopped and jumped up out of the bed and left me alone. So did Angie.

My memory comes and goes. I can't really say if Cliff got Angie. After all, he promised me that if I wouldn't tell anyone that he would leave my sisters alone. I found out when I was grown that he had told the same stuff to Deena. How many other little girls did he treat the same way? And I wonder about Cliff's own daughters by his other wife. Did he. . .

Chapter 5

---Deena---

What's that, Jack?

Did my mother take drugs or medication? Did she! Oh, hell yes. You had better believe it. Always! Always!

When my little brother was born, I was six years old, it was January...er...I was five years old. It was January of '76 when my little brother, Frank, was born. And, if they weren't married when he was born...my mother may have been pregnant when she got married. I remember when they got married. My mother dropped us off at my father's house. She and Cliff were on their way to get married. I was not happy, nor were any of the other kids. There was no inside bathroom, only an old outhouse. And we had to bathe in a big old tub. My father had another woman with him, who I suppose was his wife.

Getting back to the birth of my younger brother, we—or at least I—was unaware that my mother was pregnant or that a birth was happening. Cliff got into my mother's car to go pick her up. I thought she was at a friend's house. When my mother brought my brother home, she placed him under the rumpled covers of the bed we kids slept in. When the other children had come home from school, she told us all to make the bed. When the covers were pulled back, there lay a baby boy. My mother had told no one. Just think. If one of us had just jumped on the bed the way we normally did, what would have happened?

Anyway, I was five. My brother was a baby. I was carrying him across the rear yard. There's a creek that ran through the rear yard and under the road. There was a spot where all the teenagers would hang out, back there near that creek. They would sit on the bank and drink their beer or pops and throw the bottles into the creek. I don't know if you remember back when Cokes came in liter-sized glass bottles. Yeah, you remember. But there were a bunch of them that had been broken and were lying about in the rear field. And I was carrying the baby across the back yard.

I don't know why I was keeping him, it seemed like I always kept him. The baby was always with me. I mean, I took care of him, changed his diapers, and washed him. I fed him from the time he came home. Frank was pretty much mine. And I was five years old. Why in *hell* would you let a five-year-old babysit an infant? I mean, can you say 'negligence'?

But, anyway, I was carrying him across the back yard and I stepped in the bottom of one of those Coca Cola broken glass bottles and cut my foot really bad. Almost cut it off. And I did good—I held onto the baby. I was so proud of myself. The first thing that I guess that I remember about myself, was that I was I felt more grown-up because I never cried, never yelled, never anything. I was afraid that I would awaken the baby. I pulled my foot out of the bottle, walked into the house, put the baby down into his crib, and walked up to the door to my mother's bedroom. Her bedroom was off the living room, had louvered doors, you know, the kinds that are held shut by magnets. I knocked on her door and told her that I had cut my foot. She got really mad at me and told me to go find my oldest brother. This whole time, if you could see the blood, it was just incredible. I went outside and found my brother. He came back inside and told her that, 'No, mother, you need to see this.' When she got up and looked at the cut, she started screaming, because the bone was showing, it was cut that deep. My mother took me to the hospital, and on the way to the hospital she told me what they were going to do to my foot, that they were going to put stitches in my foot, and if I didn't cry, she would buy me ice cream on the way home.

    Well, we were so poor that ice cream at that time was a big deal. Plus I was five years old, so ice cream was a big deal. So, I went in there, and they took the biggest needle I have ever seen and numbed my foot. Then they put stitches in and all that. And on the way home—and I never cried—you know, and I couldn't believe it, but I never cried. Anyway, she didn't buy me ice cream and I was pissed off, because she went to the drug store and bought my prescription and I never took the first pain pill. She slept a lot after that. That was the first time that I actually remember seeing my mother taking pills, knowing that they were supposed to be for me for the pain. She knew that they were for me, and I couldn't figure out what. I knew that my foot hurt like hell and there's mother taking my pills.

But I have never been so upset. She hurt my feelings. She didn't buy me any ice cream, not any at all.

I felt like I was so grown up 'cause I got the baby inside, and I didn't wake the baby up, and I didn't cry the whole time. Right now, if I cut my foot like that, I'd probably scream like a wounded animal.

I remember that my mother was a waitress for a period of time, working at a restaurant called 'The Blue Mist' in Asheboro. Sometimes I would be taken along with her. The reason I remember was because this was a local hang-out for professional wrestlers. You know, like Andre the Giant, Rick Flair, Ricky Steamboat and others. They would always come in to eat when they were in the area.

~ * ~

It wasn't long after Frank was born that we moved to a two-story house, a grey two-story house on Dixie Drive, in Ramseur. It couldn't have been long after he was born, because before the move I was still walking to school, and I was still in early school. After we moved there, I started the first grade again, and as the distance from school was a little further, I was able to ride the school bus.

We moved into this house and there was no heat. There was a fireplace, and upstairs were bedrooms with other fireplaces. That's how old this house was. The boys had one bedroom, and the girls had a second, but we all ended up sleeping in the same room—all of us, his kids and her kids, and the two of them. I slept in a crib with my oldest sister. I guess it had to be Frank's crib.

Just to stay warm in that house, we would... uh.. There was, like I said, a fireplace.. They would pull all the beds into that one room, or make pallets on the floor. I just remember sleeping in the bed with my sister, in that crib, and her being, you know, ticked off because she was older and pissed off because she had to sleep in a crib with her little sister. And, you know, of course, I was wetting the bed every night, so that didn't make her real happy either.

And as far as the sexual molestation? Cliff and Michael really ramped it up in that gray house. When I say ramped it up, it was at least to or three times every week and usually more often than that. I would often try to fight Michael, to bite him or to punish him somehow. Sometimes, I was able to bite him. But he was a lot bigger than I was, and would beat me terribly every time that I resisted.

Cliff, at that time, was working nights for Roadway Trucking in Kernersville, North Carolina.

And the nights he worked.... He worked a weird schedule, like four nights on and three off and then three on and four off, that sort of thing. The nights he worked, mother would drive him to Kernersville and then she would drive back home and then to her job. That was when they started looking for a place in Kernersville, to avoid the long drive. Before the roads were as complete as they are today, it would take as much as an hour and a half to make the trip.

Cliff had no driver's license. He had been an over-the-road truck driver for Roadway, but he had received so many driving under the influence tickets that even in the forgiving times of the 1970s, the State finally took his license away. That didn't stop him from driving, but since there was only one car, usually my mother would drive.

It was in that gray house that Cliff's drinking really came into play. Because, before, I guess during the whole dating era with my mother, he didn't really want her to know how much he drank, or whatever. But anyway, he really started drinking a lot.

It was a *big* old house. And he would come up the stairs, if it were summer time; I think we only lived there, like, maybe a year. But if it was warm, the girls slept upstairs in a bedroom and the boys slept upstairs in another bedroom, and Cliff slept downstairs with my mother. There were three bedrooms upstairs, if I'm not mistaken...... anyway, there was like a.... I don't know if you remember, but in the old two-story houses built like this, where the stairs would go up, there was a space underneath that people used for storage. That's where Cliff would take me. We would be into that place, and I kept thinking, *Mother's got to hear this*, but she would never, never wake up. And I guess a large part of that may have been because she seemed to be taking a lot of pills every night. But could she have been taking that many? I just couldn't understand what was going on, why I was being abandoned. It seemed like I was so alone.

There was a big old tree in the yard. That's where Cliff staged his 'cook-out;' some cookout. He had an old oil drum that someone had cut in half, and he used that to burn some food. But, mostly, he drank.

I remember that Cliff seemed to be working the night shift, because he was home most days, and he had the weekends off. That gave him a lot of time for drinking. The average drinking day for Cliff began as soon as he got up at six o'clock in the morning and it lasted all day, two and three cases of beer. By seven o'clock in the evening, he was completely tanked. That was when he and my mother would begin fighting. Not arguing, but fighting—physically fighting.

Cliff would accuse my mother of taking drugs and stealing. And he was right. My mother was a thief. Once, she and Cliff found a checkbook and wrote checks to Helig-Myers Furniture—bought all new furniture. And there were other occasions.

Cliff had a sister who had married a fairly well-off man who had bought her a very nice, large diamond ring. When she came visiting, the ring went missing. After she had left, Cliff ransacked my mother's belongings, and found the ring. He beat her with his fists and was kicking her. We kids jumped between them, trying to stop the fighting. Cliff was so tanked it was a wonder that he could even fight. But he got hold of a gun, threatened to kill all of us.

There were a lot of times that he would shoot the gun, scaring all of us. We would have to climb out through the windows and run and hide until the police would come and get him; maybe the neighbors would calm him down or call the police. Then we would go back into the house and go to bed. Afterwards, he would come and get me, or my sister. All the time, the same damn thing!

Up until about thirty minutes before time for my mother to get home, Cliff would be in reasonably calm condition. But by the time my mother came home, Cliff would have become dark and sullen, in a deep funk. When my mother would arrive, she would look at him and then shout, 'What the hell did they do today?'

She would line us up and beat the hell out of us. Cliff would try to stop her, and that would just lead to another fight between them. It seemed like every time they were together, it was a fight; Cliff with his alcohol and my mother with her pills.

Cliff always took good care of his own kids when they came around. He would make sure that they ate first, and got all they wanted before my siblings and I could eat. I guess he was afraid they would go back and tell their mother if he didn't take extra good care of them.

That old big old tree that was out in the back yard? That's where I found out there was no Santa Claus. We would often climb that tree and one day Michael was climbing ahead of me. He was wearing cut-off shorts and saw me looking up. He pulled the shorts aside to show me that he was not wearing underwear and made me give him oral sex—again; and in a tree, in plain sight, for Christ's sake!

"What are you waiting for?" he said. "Santa Claus to come rescue you? There ain't no Santa Claus."

And I guess he was right.

Cliff would get really drunk on Christmas Eve. If we had any presents, it would only be one or two, and Cliff would make us open the presents on Christmas Eve, even though we would beg him to let us wait for Christmas Day. He really was a monster.

~ * ~

I had thought that the ride on the school bus would be better than walking to school every day. It was a really long walk for a five-year-old child to go to the schoolhouse, and the trip to the school from the gray house was even longer. It didn't take very long before I realized that I was wrong about riding the bus.

There was a guy on the school bus—it was K-12—and this guy was in the twelfth grade. I can't tell you his name right now, if I had to. Every day, when I got on the school bus, he got on the bus after me. No matter where I sat, he would always sit in the seat with me. I was in the first grade. I went to school every day with his hands in my pants. Every day! He would tell me stupid stories about when a woman was aroused, you could put a lit cigarette inside her and she wouldn't feel it. Just,,,, just all kinds of crazy stuff, you know?

Lighted cigarette? Grown woman? Aroused? My God, what kind of fool was he. I was just close to six years old. Aroused? How can you arouse a baby?

Felt it? Damn right I felt it—every single time I felt it—brutal, grabbing hands, groping and tearing! And they tore me often; my panties were frequently full of blood. And I was almost always sore. Feel it? Aroused? Shit!

It was...uh... *every* day. So I started, you know, cause I wet the bed, I started to stop washing. Maybe if I smelled bad, he would leave me alone. That didn't work. He didn't care.

Until I got a note, you know. I was the 'stinky' kid. My mother began raising hell at me because I wasn't washing before I went to school. And whenever my mother needed a baby-sitter, her friend, Becky (she was such a sweetheart). She was such a sweet woman. She always treated us like we were gold. It was always fun to go to her house when it was just her. I don't remember what Raymond did for a living, but he would be gone sometimes. I always looked forward to going over there. She taught me to crochet, and we would sit up at night, and....She never let us watch T.V. We would always do, like, arts and crafts. Stuff like that—stuff that I never got to do at home. She liked to make those little (I don't know if you remember them or not)..she liked to make those crochet covers that go over toilet paper with a doll stuck down in them. She taught me how to do that.

But, she had a son. This is the time where....This is a time when outhouses were still fairly prominent in and around that area. They weren't used anymore but they were still standing on a lot of the property.

And her son, Raymond.... he had to be seventeen or eighteen years old... and he would force me to go into the outhouse with him and would have sex with me in the outhouse. And I.... to this day, I still can't get near one. I just can't get near one.

His father is the father of my nephew. Raymond Senior got my sister pregnant when she was fifteen. And that's how she got pregnant. I don't know how long it had been going on with him, but Junior was the one that would seek me out when I was over there.

Cliff's brother, Francis, came over. And he was in the military? Was he in the Army? I think ..... When we were living in the gray house, and he had gotten out of the military he came over. And for some reason, he had...uh... People who worked for the telephone company used to climb the telephone poles manually. I don't know if you remember the spikes they would strap to the insides of their thighs. He had a set of those, you know, and, of course, all of the grown-ups were drunk. We were having another cook-out. Yeah. You know. The beatings would commence soon.

Francis went up the telephone pole, and I don't know why in the hell he did it, but he was as drunk as a three-eyed squirrel. But he was coming back down the telephone pole on his spikes, and he slipped and he fell. He had huge splinters all in his legs. They took him to the hospital, got him all cleaned up, and then they brought him home.

Well, all of the young'uns...... And the party was still going on, because God forbid the party stopped. Okay? And of course, he.... they put him upstairs in the bed, and he was still drinking and eating his pain pills. He had to have been; because he was so f...... He was really messed up.

But I would take him beers because that was our job. We were the 'beer runners'. And there was a lot of beer. There was a lot of running to be done. Cliff could drink two cases himself, Francis could put away two and one-half. It was like a contest between the two of them. So I would be taking beer up to Francis. Then, he got drunk and he got horny. When I would take a beer up to him, it would take me a while. He would have me adjust this, and adjust that. And, eventually, as the night wore on, you know, Cliff got drunker, and I don't know what my mother was doing. It may have been that she was downstairs trying to referee a fight. But, Francis would make me get him off while he was just lying there—both ways. Oral sex and hands, and you know. He never actually penetrated me, Francis never did, but it was always a lot of touching, a lot of oral sex, every time he came around. You know. And he eventually got sent to prison for it. He was doing it to his own kids, too. And they called the police on him. That's where he still is, as a matter of fact, if he's not dead.

That's about all that I can remember about the time that we lived in Ramseur, but my mother and Cliff were neither happy about the long drive every morning nor every night. So, they were looking for another house.

Anyway, we lived in Ramseur until 1978, before Cliff and my mother found a place for us to live in Kernersville. And if you think Ramseur was Hell on Earth, just keep reading.

---Starla---

You know, if you expect my memory to be sharp, and that I can recall as much as Deena, you are shit out of luck. I just can't remember everything. Much of it is just kind of foggy, lost back there somewhere. But I'll do the best I can.

The thing I remember is it seemed like every grown man and every teen-aged boy wanted to put his penis in my vagina or in my mouth—or both. And they wanted to share me with their friends. And they did.

I didn't have anyone that I could tell, and it just went on and on and on. After a while, I learned about "pot" and smoking marijuana really made things seem better. Taking pills, snorting cocaine also helped. The more, the merrier. By now I was eight or so and already smoking pot every day, thanks to the men and boys who were screwing me. Sometimes they would give me the drugs to keep me quiet. And it worked. I didn't tell anyone—not ever. Until now.

I know that Deena is either telling you or has told you about how they kept after both of us. And they scored, over and over and over. All I can do is to repeat that grown men chose young innocent girls as their sexual targets. That ain't right! Those sons-of-bitches should have to pay for what they did to us! But they won't. Nobody cares.

The only thing the men wanted to do was to stick their dirty old penises in us and the only thing my momma wanted to do was to beat us up. And it happened every day—the rape and the beatings. What a childhood!

Want to know what to give a fourteen-year-old girl for a present? How about a baby? Ain't that a bitch?

Yeah, I got pregnant when I was fourteen and had a baby when I was fifteen. And the father of the baby was Raymond. Raymond E_____. I don't care if you put his name on a billboard.

His son had already been messing with me and so had he. Like father, like son. Just like Cliff and his two sons, Michael and Robert. When we moved to Kernersville, I thought everything was going to be okay.

Raymond stayed away from me for a while and then he started coming around again. And he would take me. He would tell my momma that he was taking me shopping. I couldn't understand why my momma would let that happen. She knew that I didn't go shopping. I never came home with anything. And I never had any money to go shopping with anyway.

Raymond would take me to a motel, screw me until he got tired, and then take me back home.

My momma came home one day and looked at Angie, my older sister, who still lived there. Angie had not hung out a load of clothes to dry, so my momma told Angie to get the hell out of her house. But, before that, she had met this man named Dennis. She had kicked Cliff out and was now fooling around with Dennis.

Well, she had already got rid of my brother, Dean. That was okay with me because I always had a grudge against Dean. After all, he was my brother and he was old enough to know what was going on. He had made no effort to protect me, and I hated him for that. But, I guess that he just wanted to get out like everybody else, and he had when he turned eighteen.

Like I said, my momma came home one day and looked at Angie, my older sister who still lived there. Angie had not hung out a load of clothes to dry, so my momma told Angie to get the hell out of the house. I was raising hell. I had already lost Dean. She told me to get out and Angie said that I could come out there with her, and I did. I left.

Cliff had begun messing with me again, but at the time I got pregnant, it was only Raymond Senior. After I found out that I was going to have a baby, I didn't know whether to laugh or cry, or whether to kill the baby or myself. It started growing and I didn't know what to do. I didn't want to tell anyone once I found out that I was pregnant, and I didn't. So there was no prenatal care and I didn't have any idea about how to take care of myself or what to do. I had moved back in with my momma and was scared to tell her.

Eventually, the baby came to be the best part of my life. But having the baby was really difficult. And my momma was no help. When she found out that I was pregnant, she wanted to throw me out of the house. Screaming, shouting and beating. I was about seven months pregnant when everybody found out. The baby had already started moving and everything. Not even Dennis defended me. When momma started her tirade on me, only my sisters stood up for me, but there was little they could do.

When my momma took me to the hospital, she just dumped me out in the parking lot and drove away. I had to check in by myself, and have the baby by myself. That hurt me a lot. It seemed that I was always crying.

I don't remember much about the hospital, just that having the baby was a lot of pain, but when they put him in my arms, he was mine, all mine. The first thing I owned in my life. And I was not being raped by a bunch of men. On second thought, I guess the hospital wasn't that bad, except for being alone—and scared.

A lot of people suggested that I give the baby up, but I resisted. I just wasn't going to do that. Not to my kid.

Before the baby came, my momma had allowed me to move back into the house but with the understanding that I wasn't going to be there when the baby came. She had declared that she wasn't going to raise another kid. I just didn't know what to do. Barely fifteen and soon to be the mother of a child, and with no home.

Frank, my younger brother, was there and he was little. Frank was always little. He knew that I was pregnant. I needed to take a shower, but I was embarrassed. My belly was huge.

One day I was standing over at Bob and Pat's, a neighbor. I still went over there although they had kicked me out when I got pregnant. And I was standing over there when my water broke. I didn't know what in the hell was going on. I went in the bathroom, and it kept coming and coming.

My momma was over at Dennis' house. Pat told me to go back home and call my mom. So I went back home, and water was still coming out of me. I called my momma (I think Deena was there) and I think she was the only girl that was there. My momma wanted to know what in the hell was going on. I wasn't having any labor pains.

My momma told me to lie on the couch and to put a towel under me so that my water wouldn't stain the sofa. So I laid down on the couch and the water kept coming out of me.

She eventually came home the next morning and took me to the hospital. She didn't go in, just dropped me off and drove away. Angie was in school; my brothers were in school. I begged my momma to stay with me just until I had the baby, but she wouldn't stay.

They took me into the ward, the emergency ward, and all of the water had stopped coming out. They had a little monitor on my son and they were watching his heart. They couldn't find a heartbeat.

The nurse asked me, "Can you feel that?" prodding me.

I said, "No." She asked me if I was having labor pains and I told her no, there was no pain. I asked them to call the school so that Angie could be there when I woke up, but they wouldn't.

They had lost my son's heartbeat and one of them said, "We're going to have to take the baby. Do you want to be put out or what?"

I said, "Yes, put me out." And they did.

When I woke up I could hear a baby screaming but I couldn't see it. I couldn't see anything. But I heard him crying.

They kept telling me, "Look at your baby. Look at your baby" The nurses kept saying, "Look at your baby. You've got a beautiful child."

I said, "Well, I can't see him." I really couldn't see him.

They said, "Well, your eyes are open."

But I said, "Well, I can't see my baby."

"Wait a few minutes." After a little while I could see again. Finally, the picture was clear up there. I had a beautiful child; light haired, blue eyes. He was beautiful.

Momma never showed up.

I was glad that I didn't give him up.

There was a conspiracy going on, that's what I called it. They were trying to adopt my baby out. And I wouldn't let it happen.

A friend of mine told me not to sign no papers. He must have known what he was talking about. My momma had made arrangements with Rick, her brother, and his wife to adopt the baby. But it was up to me. The arrangements had already been made, but I didn't know anything about it, until Chris told me about it later.

Well, it was time for me to go home, but I had nowhere to go. I tried to move in with Angie, but she didn't have much space at all. I had just turned sixteen, so I guess that made Angie barely seventeen. There was eleven months difference between our birthdays. Angie was living with a woman called Belinda at the time. After I stayed there a about a week and then I got evil. The woman told me that I had to go.

So I went up to the town. Social services and all that didn't give me anything; no place to stay, no job, no money. The only thing they did for me was, well, something. What's that word, emancipation? They helped me get emancipated from my momma, but that still didn't give me a place to live.

Well, by then I was already staying with a friend of mine named Roscoe, his momma, and his brother. Well, guess what? Put out or get out. I had to have sex with both of the males, one grown man and the other in his late teens. Out of the frying pan and into the fire.

Roscoe had a son. Roscoe worked in tobacco. When I was twelve, I worked in the same field. One day, he got me up on the tractor, and there I was driving the tractor. I was having a ball.

Well, then he took off on the tractor with me hanging on. He went around the corner of a barn, stopped and got me off. Roscoe pulled off my panties, laid me down on the ground and spread motor oil on me—then he screwed me.

Anyway, I was living in his basement. And he would keep coming down and get me. I don't know if his wife knew, but he just kept on screwing me. And so did his brother.

Chapter 4

---Deena---

When I first learned that my mother and Cliff had found a house and that we were going to move to Kernersville for sure, my first feelings were of fear. I was terrified. We were going to move away from everything I knew, everything that I had become accustomed to, everything that had surrounded me—a new school, a new town, all new people, and just that many more adults who would only want one thing.

Alcohol. Alcohol was always present. When we were packing up, Cliff would sit and get drunk. And every time he got tanked, he got horny and would want to screw me or make me give him oral sex.

I don't remember a lot about the move itself, because I didn't want to. I didn't want to go. I was scared. I was leaving what I knew. I was leaving my grandma, you know?

We moved into a house on Morton Drive in Kernersville when I was seven. It was a little three-bedroom one-story house, and you might think that Ramseur was out of sight, out of mind. Far from it.

After we moved to Kernersville, we would go back to the Asheboro-Ramseur area a lot to visit. Cliff had gotten hold of an enormous old Cadillac. I hate that kind of car to this day. You couldn't give me one, not even a new one. Not even if it were completely free.

Anyway, we would all be in the car. My mother would be driving and Cliff was always sitting in the back seat. Although it was a large car, it was tight when all of us were inside. Because of the number of passengers, and because I was one of the smallest, of course I would wind up sitting on Cliff's lap the entire trip, both going and coming. And it was a long trip, at least an hour and maybe even more. And of course, his hands were in my crotch all the way, rubbing and twisting; rubbing me and then rubbing himself; rubbing himself with his fingers in my vagina until he got off.

And no one noticed?

What made it even worse was the car's exhaust system was old and leaky, and the odor came into the interior of the car. Can you imagine being nauseous and being molested at the same time for an hour or more by someone that you just hated? And you were still a child?

I started in the second grade after we moved to Kernersville—Kernersville Elementary. I was still seven, and would be eight in December.

Whenever I got to Kernersville Elementary, I was just blowing them away in school. I was....er... because it always came naturally to me. Guess it was because school was a refuge for me.

When I was in the second grade, they tested me and they wanted to skip me from the second to the fourth grade. Okay.

Well, when I went home that day, that was, of course, cause for celebration. You know. Whip out the alcohol. Right? It was a Saturday that I had to take the test on, and I took the test that Saturday morning, and scored very highly. It was, you know—everybody was excited, but it was more a party for the grown-ups than it was for me. I.. uh... I did the thing I always do—I ran the beers, you know, trying to stay out of everybody's way. Performed like a puppet on a string.

That night, my mother went to bed, and so did everyone else. And Cliff got me up, and was telling me how smart I was and how pretty I was, you know. The same old thing—he made me give him a blowjob (Oral sex, for any of you who don't know what a blowjob is). Yeah, congratulations to me! Good job.

It made me so angry that I told them that no, I didn't want to skip a grade. It turned me completely off, killed all my excitement.

When I was in the third grade, the teacher told my mother that I ... that I was bored. And I was;

I was bored with school. So they tested me again, and put me into the academically gifted program. So instead of going to Kernersville, I went to Walkertown Elementary.

And, whenever they did that, it was cause for celebration once again, you know. Let's bring out the beer and have sex with the kids!

It ramped up again when we moved up here. I don't know if it was because Cliff felt like once he was away from the people that knew us that he could get away with more, I guess. Or what I don't know. But his drinking was just awful. And I just don't mind anyone drinking, but he would really drink. And then he would get angry and want to fight. And then he wanted to fuck. Excuse my language, but that's the way it went. And I apologize that I have to be so blunt.

Just because I don't say in every other sentence that sex took place, that doesn't mean that it didn't—at least once a week, and on many occasions as often as once a night or a day. And sometimes more than once. If it was not Cliff, then it was

Michael, or a friend of one or the other of them. They kept telling me that was what a female was for, even a little girl. I suppose that I heard it so often, and from so many different adults, that I began to believe it. A woman was supposed to always be ready for any male, for anything, and was not supposed to object. If she objected, or if she told someone, then she was not a good girl, and everyone would know that she was not a good girl. What you were supposed to do was just keep your mouth shut, wait until they were finished, and then go on about your life. Right!

But he.... uh...every good thing that happened to us was celebrated the same way—everything.

Christmas. Christmas was always interesting at our house. It was a trip. You never knew what the hell was going to happen at Christmas. I never looked forward to Christmas. I don't remember a time when I was excited about Christmas. I never looked forward to it until I moved out. And now Christmas is a big deal for me. All the holidays are a big deal for me.

I was nine, probably, eight or nine, second or third grade, I forget. And Christmas was coming. I don't think it was quite Christmas Eve, maybe three or four days before Christmas, but Cliff was there. He was off work. I dreaded it when he was off work. It was always the same. First the drinking, then the fighting, and then, you know, someone had to get him off before he would pass out and go to sleep. Guess who that someone was?

Anyway, it was a few days before Christmas and we were in the house. Cliff's kids were there, too. Cliff was, and had been, drinking up a storm, and was sitting on the couch. He told me to come sit down beside him. What do you do? You go sit down. So, I went and sat down beside him. He put his arm around me and told me that he was going to adopt me. He wanted me to be 'his child'.

He had been telling my mother that he was going to adopt me; that he was going to adopt us all.

I made the mistake of saying that I already have a daddy. That caused a huge uproar. He flipped way out. And he said, basically, that 'if you don't want be here, if you don't like what I do for you, then you've got to leave;' you've got to do this, you've got to do that. And, I was eight years old, you know? What did I know? And basically, I just wanted to know what would happen with my real dad. Am I not going to have him? You know? I was just curious.

    Cliff started having a fit, slinging shit around, and went in the kitchen and started taking. . .why is it that when he would get pissed, or when my mother would get pissed, they would go in the kitchen and they would pull *all* of the dishes out of every cabinet and make the kids wash them. I was short. I had to have a stool to even get to the sink. You know? But for some stupid reason or another, it was always the same damn thing; they would pull all of the dishes out and make us wash them. And if we didn't wash them good, they would start slinging them against the wall, you know, there was glass everywhere, everything's broken, everybody's screaming, everybody's crying. And Cliff was going to spank me. And my mother got in the way, or something. I forget. And he pushed her down against the counter in the kitchen and when she fell she cracked her head on the side of the counter.

Her head was bleeding. And then we jumped on him, and when I say we, it was all five of us kids who jumped on him. And he pushed us off and went into his room and got his gun. He came down the hall with his shotgun; he was going to shoot everybody. He flung it at me and missed, and my mother started screaming at us to run; his kids were there, too, you know. We ran into our bedroom, locked the door, pushed the bed in front of the door, and then jumped out the window. We were all barefooted, it was December, and it was cold. We all ran out into the woods. A neighbor across the road, Jimmy, heard the commotion, and came outside. He saw us running. He walked into the woods, trying to find us. And of course, we didn't know who the hell he was, so we didn't answer when he called. He finally found us and took us to his house.

That was the first time I ever saw a SWAT team. I found out that they really did have a police force called the SWAT Team. Before, I couldn't believe there actually was one, because you only saw it on T.V. Well, they finally calmed him down and everything. I don't know what the hell it was about the late 'seventies, but we went back into the house that night, you know? Nobody thought that maybe we ought to get the kids the hell out of there. So we went back into the house and my mother went to bed. So did the rest of us. And Cliff came and got me, again. Everybody was asleep. I guess it was my turn because I was the one who asked about my real daddy.

  The SWAT Team was real cool. They jumped out of the truck with guns, and surrounded the whole house, and had the bullhorn going, you know, and Cliff figured out that, 'Well, I'd better walk my happy ass outside, or I'm going to die.' So he walked outside, they took the gun away from him, and he explained it, and after we went back into the house, we had to clean everything up. And the police talked to my mother, and she said that everything was fine and that Cliff could stay. And we cleaned the kitchen, and she went to bed. Everyone went to bed, and then Cliff got horny—again. It disgusted me; it always disgusted me; made me want to vomit. But, I knew that if I did, not only would I have to clean it up, but that I would be beaten again.

You know, that was the Christmas I got my diary. It sure was. My oldest sister gave me that diary, and she told me when she gave it to me...because it was rare for any of us to have enough money to buy a gift for the other ones, you know.... And my gift to them, like for their birthday and stuff, I always used to do a book report for them for school. My oldest sister could never spell, love her to death, but she'll never learn to spell, and my other sister would never enjoy any kind of schoolwork. And I always loved it. So I would always do that for them. It came easy for me.

I remember thinking, you know, that she saved her money and bought this for me. So, it was very special. Very, very special.

There was a little boy that lived on the road behind us, (the neighborhood was like a horse shoe) and his name was Jimmy. This had to be in 1979. I was eight years old. And Jimmy was my boyfriend. I was in love.

His family was Seventh Day Adventists, so he only had certain times he could play, you know. They couldn't go out on the weekends. They were very strict. They had some strict rules.

Tobacco fields were everywhere at that time. I don't know if you remember how prevalent they were, but what we used to do is we would go out and play in tobacco fields. We knew enough not to knock the plants over, we knew enough not to damage the fields. We never got into trouble for anything like that. Plus, we were working in tobacco in the summertime. That's probably where my sister got the money, as a matter of fact, to buy that diary for me.

Jimmy gave me my very first kiss. And I was so excited. I was so happy. I went home, because I thought, I've got something that I was going to write in *my* diary, I was so excited. Something very private to write in my new diary. . .

In the diary itself, I was writing that Jimmy kissed me. And I wrote a lot..... about things we might do together. Things that I had no ideas about...not that I had no idea, but a child at that age certainly should not have any idea of. I was writing about having sex with him and all the different things that I was going to do to him because I knew how to do it. And I was very explicit about it because it never occurred to me that I shouldn't write such things, or that anyone might read that. It just didn't occur to me.

Well, my mother found that diary. And I was in my bedroom, on top of the bed. I forget what I was doing, but my mother walked into the bedroom and she had the diary—*my* diary in her hand.

You know the kind of feeling you get when someone punches you right in the pit of your stomach? That's ......as soon as I saw the diary in her hand—I knew.

My mother never cleaned our room. Okay? So I had it hid—under the mattress. So she had to have gone looking for it in our room. And first, I thou... first of all, I was pissed! You know, I had no privacy whatsoever. And that was mine! The only thing that was just mine.

And she had read it. She beat the shit out of me. I mean, beat the shit out of me. She accused me of everything in the book, you name it.

You know, it didn't really dawn on me at that time, but it did later when I had grown up enough. Why didn't she stop and think for a moment; about, 'Who told my child about oral sex? Who told my child about intercourse because she had never told me? I knew about all this stuff, I had written it down, so obviously somebody had. . .but she got angry at me. Just for writing it down!

I thought she was going to kill me. I honestly did. She beat me so bad that I thought she was going to kill me. She grounded me for the summer. So, I never wrote anything down after that. That taught me a lesson real quick.

These words with you, Jack, will be the first thing that has been written down since then.

That made me really hate her, you know. I hated her. 'Cause she never protected me, you know. I guess she blamed it all on me—especially for writing it down.

That same summer, my sister must have been twelve. Yeah, I was eight and one-half, around that age, and she was twelve. Everybody took off, to go back to Ramseur or Franklinville, or somewhere in that area, and for once, I didn't have to go. I didn't have to sit in Cliff's lap. For once I was oh so excited about that.

My sister was supposed to watch me. Well, she was twelve, and as soon as they were out of sight, she was out the door and gone. She left me at home, by myself. We were supposed to clean the house. Well, she came back. My sister came back about an hour or maybe an hour and a half before the rest of them were supposed to be home, right? I guess she was thinking that we could clean the whole house in an hour and a half.

We tried. But, you know, an eight year old and a twelve-year-old. How clean is it going to be?

My mother came into the house and saw that the house wasn't clean. She pulled the electrical cord out of a table lamp. Just unplugged it from the wall and yanked the cord completely out of the back of the lamp. And she started beating on me with that.

I don't know if you've ever been whipped with a switch, beat until you bleed, but it's nothing like an electrical cord. And....uh.... Cliff got it away from her, pulled it out her hands. He was strong.

So she pulled curtains down from the window in the living room, took the curtains off the metal rod and started beating me with the rods. Those sheet metal rods, every time she would hit me, would bend. And it would cut me.

How do you do that to a kid?

How do you make them bleed like that?

That night, after she went to bed, I was lying in my bed. I was still bleeding. Cliff came in there and got me and took me into the bathroom. He put peroxide on my back and on my legs. And, of course, I had to take my clothes off. So, I guess he felt like I hadn't had enough that day. He made me give him oral sex—in the bathroom, of all places. I couldn't even think. My back and my legs were hurting so bad.

I began to get pissed off at everything.

How do you do that?

It's likely my sister got into trouble also, but I don't remember that. I just remember what happened to me.

What was it about me? You know, that's what I used to think all the time. What in the hell is wrong with me? There must be something wrong with me. How else could I be a target—for everyone? Or so it seemed from the time I was four.

When I was in the fourth grade, I started an A.G. Program, (academically gifted program). At that time, I was still wetting the bed, you know, because at that time, we didn't know there was any problem with my bladder.

Cliff just wouldn't leave me alone. And I know I would be lying in bed and hear him messing with my sister. He told me often that if I would do what he wanted me to do that he would leave my sisters alone. But sometimes, I would try to pretend to be asleep. But then I felt guilty, about not being able to help my sister. And it was right there in the same bedroom.

He.... When I got up in the mornings, I started to not bathe; I didn't want him touching me anymore. But he didn't care.

I got another note from my fourth grade teacher that I brought home. She had pulled me over to the side, and started telling me that, you know, if I didn't start washing that she wasn't going to let me back into her class. Oh, God. And I really wanted to tell her, 'You don't have a clue,' but I didn't.

I forget what I said to her, but I smarted off to her, and she held me by my arm. Her grip was so tight, that her fingernails dug into my flesh, and so I had scratches and bruises on my arm. When I went home, I took the note home to my mother. And when she saw my arm, of course, that was a big thing, you know.

My mother went to the school, and. . .it was the damndest thing, you know, when the public was watching, she was the most defensive person, you know? She was going to fight every battle for me, if somebody was looking.

That summer was when she finally took me to the doctor, and the doctor asked me. . .because they. . .it got to where I finally couldn't have anything to drink after six o'clock in the evening. They were just trying to..... they were tired of me wetting the bed.

I went to the doctor, and the doctor told my mother that I had an immature bladder, about twenty-five percent as large as it should have been at that age. And he told her that 'there was no way that she could help this, she just can't help it'.

And on the way home, I kept saying, "Okay, you know, where's my apology? Damn it, you beat the hell out of me. You made me stand on the front porch with 'pissy' clothes on my head, you know. Where's my apology?"

She never said a word—never said anything.

They scheduled a hospital visit. I was going in for surgery. I went to the High Point hospital. I don't know the status of Baptist or Forsyth hospitals at that time, but for some reason, I had to go to the High Point hospital.

She took me over there, got me signed in and everything, and I got into the little hospital gown. Surgery was scheduled for six o'clock the next morning. And, then she left.

I was nine years old, and she left. I can't imagine leaving a child..... I couldn't do that. My son is eleven, and I couldn't do that.

And I laid there in the hospital and cried and cried. I was so scared. I had no idea what in the hell they were going to do to me the next day. You know, they were talking about putting a tube in me... and stretching my bladder, and I was alone. No one to explain it all.

She just left. And before she left, I was trying to talk her into staying. I told her my stomach hurt, hoping she would stay. She told me just to roll over and lay on my stomach, it would feel better.

That wasn't fair. She never cared about me. She never has. Or at least if she does, she cares so much more about her damn self.

~ * ~

Francis started coming back over. We had a garden, out by the...I forget the name of the road, but it's across town. Somebody that they knew owned the property. And because there were so many kids, you know....we were *poor*. So we had this big garden in the summer time. We had to go over and work in the garden. I mean, it was *Big*!. We would work in it all day. And, of course, Cliff would sit on a bucket and drink. My mother was at work, I assume.

One day, he got a wild hair. He was going to take us to Belews Creek to go swimming. That was okay. It was a treat for everybody. We didn't get to go swimming very often. So.... everybody was out swimming. Me and Frank were.....and I mean we were the youngest ones.

Cliff took me around the corner, or actually, there wasn't a corner—he took off me into the woods.

Nothing was ever good. Nothing was. . .if something good was about to happen, you knew who had to pay for it.

I knew that I had to pay for it because he was going to get drunk. And I knew that I would have to do something for him.

My God, it hurt so bad! He. . .uh. . .he made me hold onto a tree.

And all I had to do was yell. All my brothers and sisters would have come over there if I had just yelled. I still don't know why I didn't.

What is attractive about a nine-year-old girl? What is sexually attractive about a nine-year-old little girl? Nothing!

There was a big rock. Back over where we were swimming. And after he was done, we went back there where everybody else was. And...uh...I was sitting on that rock and semen was coming out of me, and I remember trying to hide it from everyone else. I jumped into the water and was splashing water up on the rock to wash the semen off before anyone could see. I didn't want anyone to know what was happening to me.

Always the same thing!

It was just too much. It was just way too much.

It was so disgusting. He was always telling me how pretty I was. How desirable. A child who was always crying?

After the garden.....after the garden started developing, we would go out there..... God, I mean, it was huge! We would spend all day snapping beans. Or, we would spend all day shucking corn, you know, that sort of thing.

We did it...there was a carport on the house. It was just a one-story ranch house with an attached carport instead of a garage. We would sit under the carport and snap beans, or whatever, and Cliff would sit and drink. And his buddy would come over.

I want to say...he had some sort of a funky-ass nickname. Easy, or something like that. East. That's what it was. I believe that East was his last... no, wait a minute. Not East—it was W_____. That's right. W_____. But his nickname was Shaky. They called him 'Old Shaky W_____.'

He had two sons. I forget what their names were. But, I was shucking corn, sitting on the carport steps, and they were sitting in lawn chairs on the other side of the carport—about eight, maybe ten feet away.

I don't know where the other kids were, they might have been there, but I can't remember. But Cliff was telling Shaky, you know, what he was doing to me. And, you know, the day went on, and Shaky hung around. It got dark and all the kids were playing hide and seek. And....Oh, my God! He was disgusting!

But, they watched where I went, and Shaky came and found me. He was telling me that he knew how much I liked it, how much I must have liked it, because I was doing it for my step-dad and I wouldn't have been doing it unless I liked it. And that it wouldn't take just a minute. So, he led me out into the woods and he had me give him oral sex, too.

I hated my life—just hated it and everyone in it.

And after a while, I couldn't even fight them no more. After a while, I believed them. I really believed that was all that I was good for. That all a woman was for was for sex, and that she didn't have the right to say no. Not to anyone.

No, Shaky didn't force me to have sex or oral sex with him after that. But he was always coming around and I had to sit on his lap, you know, and his hands were always in my pants, or up under my shirt. And, you know, there was nothing up my shirt. My God, I was seven or eight years old. I don't know what the hell, you know?

He would rub up against me until he got off, you know? He made me sit in his lap so that he could rub his organ against me until he ejaculated.

~ * ~

I just wanted somebody to…uh…just to be nice to me. You know? But, they all wanted the same thing.

Every time that Michael came over, it was the same damn thing. Michael….there was a song. It was his favorite song. I think it was called "The Martian Boogie." And he would play that damn song, and he would be smoking dope. And I knew as soon as that mess started, what was going to happen.

You've got to understand. When you have six kids living in a house, and the house is a small house anyway, with three girls in one room and three boys in one room and my mother and Cliff in the third bedroom, and then when his kids came over they slept on the couch or made a pallet and slept on the floor. . . anyway. . .you know as well as I do that there's not much that can go on in a house that full that you won't hear it.

I'm certain that my sisters could hear it, but it was probably happening to them, too. They couldn't do anything. How in God's name could all that be happening and my mother not know what was happening and could pretend not to hear anything? You tell me!

I slept in the living room when Michael came over. I don't know why I was sleeping in the living room, but for some reason I was. At my age now, I believe it was because something may have been happening to one or the other of my sisters in the bedroom.

I slept on the couch. And I woke up and he was on top of me. I started to say something, and he put his hand over my face, smothering me and saying, "Shut up, I'll be done in a minute. Shut up!"

So, I just lay there, until he got done.

~ * ~

One of Michael's friends that lived up on Bethel Church Road—Eddie _____ God, he was a disgusting fucking individual, excuse my fucking language. Long red hair, skinny, drug addict.... he would come over and spend the night with Michael. So, Eddie would watch. And then, he eventually would join in.

I was maybe ten, either nine or ten years old.

And that happened so many times, I can't....even....I just can't remember how many times it happened. I can't remember all the men that did that... those things to me. That's how rampant that kind of mess is.

There was another guy that lived up off---do you know where Glenn Cross is? He lived down Glenn Cross.

We used to.... There was a little patch, or tract of woods, we called it Half-Track. Kids would ride their bikes and their motorcycles around it. And there was a path...do you know where Sahabie Field is? Off of NC 150, Oak Ridge Road? No? Stigall Road?

There was a path, where you could go from the Half-Track all the way to Sahabie Field and about halfway through the woods we had built a fort out there. Well, I started smoking dope when I was nine, and that's where I would always go.

Oh, yes. I had my first marijuana when I was barely nine—stole it from my oldest brother. Just stole it from him. It was in the top drawer of his dresser, and I knew it was there. He didn't give it to me. As a matter of fact, he would have kicked my ass if he knew that I had got it. But, at least, I got it. He had a couple of them rolled up already, and so I took it. And I was not going to smoke it in the house. So I went out to the Half-Track and I smoked it out there.

I don't think my brother knows it to this day. It may have belonged to one of his friends, but I didn't care, I knew the bigger kids smoked it and I wanted to try it.

I already knew how to smoke; about inhaling and all that. I grew up around cigarettes, and in the

'70's nobody cared if you smoked, and in my family, certainly no one cared.

Yeah, I went out there, and I was crossed-eye stoned. I mean it was ridiculous. I was so dizzy that I couldn't even stand up.

Ah. . .that marijuana, the 'joint', was really something different. I only smoked half of it, and saved the other half for another time. Let me tell you, heaven!

That's right—Heaven. Moms and dads, you are going to have your hands full keeping your children away from drugs. More about that later but for now, let's just say that the reason why you will have problems is that the drugs make the user feel good. Real good.

For the first time in my entire life, all nine years of it, I felt good. God, did I feel good. And from that day, through everything, I was hooked, but good. As you will learn, if it made you feel good, I wanted it. A dope fiend? Why not? Who cared?

And then I got really paranoid because I couldn't stand up. I thought I was going to die. You know? So, I stayed out there for a long, long time. And then, after I got over being paranoid, it felt wonderful.

It felt just woonderrrrfullllll!

I didn't worry about anything. I loved it—absolutely loved it. I was glad that I had saved half of it for the next day.

And my brother still didn't know that I had taken his joint. Of course, he will now. Sorry, Dean...

He works for the police station, now. Dean was.... he always was a good kid. He dabbled on a little bit, but he never got into anything major. It might have been his or it might have been Michael's, but if I'm not mistaken it was his. And I took it from him.

And....uh.... I discovered the wonderful world of numbing your senses, because if you are messed up on anything, your problems aren't that bad. And, they're just not.

Loved smoking dope; loved smoking hash, especially, when I could get my hands on it.

Drugs were everywhere. All I had to do was to take it. I mean all of the kids had some.... Like I said, this was the late '70's, you know, and pot was everywhere. Of course, it's plentiful today, but it was everywhere back then. And it was the good shit, too.

I mean, Michael smoked it, Eddie_____ smoked it, you know. And after a while, if they were going to do what they were going to do, they had to give it to me. So, I guess I was a drug prostitute. At *ten*! Ten years old.

I tried 'speed' or 'meth' when I was ten, but it made me throw-up. I was looking for something to numb the pain, you know, not to make it more prevalent. And that's what speed did to me. On the other hand, I am certain that I tried everything that was available. And some of it was very, very good.

~ * ~

There was a guy—everybody called him "Goofy." He's dead now. He died in a car accident. I guess that Goofy was on his way to Sahabie Field and

I was out there smoking a joint. And he came over and sat down, and he was smoking it with me.

He was, oh, maybe sixteen. And.... you know. It was the same damn thing.... and I didn't fight him either.

And I remember thinking. He just tore my Mickey Mouse underwear. 'Cause I liked them, you know, and I was pissed off because he tore the underwear. I kept thinking, how am I going to hide that from my mother?

And the point I guess I'm trying to make is that eventually I just accepted anybody. I didn't fight it, I didn't say no, not anymore. If you wanted to, I let you. I mean, what could I do? That's what girls are for.

I mean, it was going to happen anyway. If it didn't happen with you, it was going to happen when I went home. And it was probably going to happen at home in any case.

I just didn't say no, not any more. And then, I felt guilty. I felt like I was trash 'cause I wasn't saying no.

Depraved? You don't know the half of it.

~ * ~

There was a bar, they called it "Fisherman's Lounge" down off Piney Grove Road. I'm sure that you have seen the pond back there, right across the street where the Pantry convenience store used to be. You know, where that Shell station is now. There was a beautiful white house down there; I mean a really beautiful big white house. I think they run a plumbing company or something out of it now. But anyway, there was a big pond down there. And if I'm not mistaken and I could be wrong but I think that the lady that we were renting our house from owned that big house. I don't believe she owns it now, but she did at that time. And there was a building beside that white house, which is where they run the plumbing company out of, but it used to be a bar. And it was called "The Fisherman's Lounge".

We would go down there and fish in that pond.

They sold beer in the bar. I don't think they had a liquor license so they didn't sell liquor, at least not legally. But they did sell a lot of beer.

Well, Cliff got in the habit of going down there, you know, and the rest of us would go down there with him. He would take us all down there, even my mother. You know, it was Family Night at the Bar. That's always a good thing—for Cliff.

He used to go down there and sit at the picnic tables outside. There were three picnic tables in front of the bar. And, I don't know if Cliff just spread the word to the guys down there or what, or if they just picked up on it somehow. But, if I sat at the picnic table, it never failed. Just like moths to a flame. Here they came.

They would come out of the bar, and sit down beside me. And tell me how pretty I was. You know? And then their hands would be in my pants.

I was sitting at a picnic table, with people all around me. They would wait, until they thought nobody was looking, and lead me around the corner of the building. And it was nasty back there. It stunk.

You've been around where people fish, and that was where they threw...that's where they cleaned their fish, and just left the garbage there.

They would either have sex with me, or make them give them oral sex, or something—whatever they wanted that night. And, you know, it was always the same. And after they were done, they would, like, buy me a Pepsi or something.

"Appreciate it," Yeah. Appreciate it.. Thanks, Ass-hole.

How could Cliff or my mother have not been aware of what was going on? There were, what, three picnic tables in the front of the bar. How can you not be aware that they're taking your kid around the corner? But then, Cliff didn't care. He was doing the same thing himself.

That's... that's always what struck me, you know? How could you not be aware of it? And I didn't even know these guys' names!

And it was the same thing at Howard's. Howard's was a bar, over off Route 66, behind the Pizza Hut. Like I said, Howard used to give us a nickel for every beer can we would pick up out of the parking lot.

So Cliff would be inside, and there were video games in there. That was something we didn't get to do very often, so we would go pick up the beer cans to have money for the video games. And....uh...Cliff would be inside drinking and I would be outside in the parking lot, picking up beer cans.

If the bathrooms were full, they would come outside to use the bathroom. Have you ever been to Howard's, Jack?

Well, at the time, there were a lot more woods around Howard's then there are now.

And I think that my fiancé used to live over in that area at one time.

I don't think Howard had any idea what was happening. Did you ever meet Lucille? You know, that club—that ball bat he always kept behind the counter, under the bar that he called "Lucille." If he had known that men were assaulting and having sex with seven and eight year old children, he would have cleaned house with Lucille.

But...uh... to the right of Howard's, when you pulled up, into the parking lot, you parked facing the building. And the door to enter was straight ahead. Over to the side was a huge tree, or there used to be. On a busy night, people just parked everywhere.

And you got 'snockered', really tanked, at Howard's. I mean, this was in the seventies. There was no limit and no one cared how drunk you got as long as you could still pay. Alright?

And it was behind that big old tree that they would take me. I'd be outside, cleaning up the beer cans. There were beer cans everywhere, all of the time. And then one of them would come outside. To go use the bathroom, I guess. And would see me, and pull me over behind that tree. And it would be the same damn thing.

I don't know if Cliff. . .I know that at the Fisherman's Lounge, Cliff had to have known. But, at Howard's, it may have been a different story, because he was inside, you know.

I hated him so bad, you know, that I always, in my mind, I accused him of telling all those men that I was outside. But, I don't know for a fact that he did that.

I don't know. I imagined that he did. But, I don't know for sure.

~ * ~

When I was. . .I'm trying to think. I wasn't quite eleven. We were working in tobacco, for some of the guys around here. And one of them had a son, named Ricky.

Ricky was about the same age as my older brother, in fact, may have been a little older. Yeah. He was sixteen or seventeen years old. He was driving.

Do you know who Kendall _____ is? Builds bikes? Kendall used to come down and work in the tobacco fields with us and hang out.

Do you know there's a waterfall right down Bethel Church Road? It was beautiful down there. I don't know who owns it now, but they used to let us go down there as long as we didn't....There were leeches in the waterfall part itself, but we dammed it off a little further down and made like a swimming hole. We used to go down there a lot. It was gorgeous down there.

Kendall and Ricky were pretty close, pretty tight. Or at least, that's the way I remember it. And Kendall had a Jeep. First Jeep I ever saw, you know, one of the Wranglers, and I thought that was the coolest damn thing I had ever seen, you know. And Kendall used to give me a ride in the Jeep. Kendall was a good guy, and I had the biggest crush on him. Here he is, this high school kid, in his Jeep, you know, and I thought, well, that was pretty cool.

But Ricky would come over and spend the night. Depending on where we were working, in what field, he would either stay at our house, he and his sister, or we would stay at their house sometimes. And I was staying at his house one night, it was right up here on Bethel Church Road, a little brick house, and I was sleeping in his sister's bedroom. His sister was not there; she was staying with a friend. As a matter of fact, she may have been staying with my sister; they were pretty close. And Ricky came in there, and it was the same thing. He kept asking me, "Do you want me to do this? Do you want me to do this?" and, I remember, I couldn't say anything. It was like I was frozen. I just couldn't say any thing, couldn't get anything out, you know? And because I couldn't say anything, he went ahead and done it. And then he left. And, I guess he went to bed, or whatever.

About two hours later, his dad came in my room, in the room that I was in, and got into the bed with me. And, of course, he started messing with me.

He put his hand in my underwear, and kept saying, "Did you wet the bed? Did you wet the bed?" And then, he called me by his daughter's name, And....I just kind of froze, you know? I didn't know what the hell...I was scared. This was twice in one damn night, I didn't know what the hell. . .

And then his wife came in the room and flipped on the light and started raising hell at him. "That's not Karen! That's not Karen!"

And then it dawned on me that he was doing this to his own kid.

It was happening every-damn-where!

Aren't there any normal parents?

~ * ~

I don't know.

It's like I told you before. It was like I walked around with a big damn target on me. Like I was a magnet.

Every time Cliff's brother came up, you know, and I'd go to bed and be asleep. Then, I'd feel somebody sitting on the bed.

I didn't want to go anywhere alone—unless I was out in the woods. I used to love to go out into the woods by myself. Of course, I was smoking dope. So...

When I was twelve.... on my twelfth birthday, for my present on my twelfth birthday . . .and I was home from school sick. You know, come to think of it, they may have just let me have a day, skip a day.

Anyway, I was home alone with Cliff. We were cleaning the carpet in the living room.

But, for my present, he told me that if I would help him clean the carpet, he would take me to Hardee's. I had never had a fast food burger in my life. So, I was excited. Alright! A big treat.

He started drinking about ten o'clock that morning, and had all of the furniture either flipped up on its side or moved out of the way. I was ....it was partly my job to... uh...we had this spot remover, you know, so I was crawling around the floor on my hands and knees, cleaning up the heavier spots, before Cliff used the steam cleaner.

The couch was turned up on its side, with the seats down. I was crawling in front of it when I heard Cliff unfasten his pants, and I had to lean over the couch. And that's what I got for my twelfth birthday.

And after we were done—after *he* was done—he took me to Hardee's. And I didn't even want anything to eat, you know.

And he kept yelling at me, "I'm not doing anything else for you, you're ungrateful," and all that kind of stuff. So I forced myself to eat the fries and the hamburger, but half way home, I threw it all up in the car.

Then, when my mother got home, she beat me because I threw up in the car. She said it was because the car stunk.

So, Happy Birthday to me! Yeah, happy, happy birthday, Deena.

~ * ~

I never even had a birthday cake until I turned twenty-one. That was the first birthday cake I ever got. My ex-husband got it for me.

By the time I was twelve, I had more knowledge about sex than....than you probably do now.

As I said, I never got to be a virgin. I never got to be a little girl. I never got to have that 'first time.' I don't know what that's like.

My schoolwork at this time was still excellent. I was acing everything. I devoured school. I hadn't yet gotten pissed. It had started boiling in me at that time, but I didn't really blow my lid until I was fifteen. Fourteen or fifteen. And by then, I was buck-ass wild.

When I was twelve, that was the year—twelve or thirteen, that was the year that my mother started going out on Cliff. I don't know if she got tired of. . .tired of every holiday being ruined, or what, but she started...she was working at Salem Leasing, and she met a man that she worked with. And.... she told me about him, because she came home one night and.... Cliff was working the night shift, and she came home and had whisker burns all over her neck. Alright?

And when she walked in the door, she told me that she had an allergic reaction. I told her, "I don't know who you think you are fooling, but I know better than that, I know where that stuff comes from." And I told flat out that I knew where that stuff came from.

Yes, at twelve. It didn't dawn on her. Duh.

And she told me that Cliff had been trying to force her to have sex with the animals—with the dogs. And I remember getting pretty pissed off, because, like, "Why would you tell me that? Why would you want me to know that?"

She kept telling me about all these things Cliff wanted her to do, you know, but she was telling me. .... .I don't know, but she was telling me a ton of things.

My two sisters, Angie and Starla, had been emancipated at that time. The neighbors that lived around—it didn't take long to clue them that there were problems at our house, because like I said every holiday we were climbing out the windows and running to the neighbor's house.

Or, and it didn't even have to be a holiday, Cliff got drunk and, you know, all the hell-raising.

Somebody called the Social Services Agency on us when I was eight. I don't know who it was, maybe one of the neighbors. But they called the Social Services office on us and a social worker came out and interviewed my mother, and then she interviewed all of us. And told us that she was going to take us out of the house, and that we would be separated. At that time, the thought of not being with my brothers and sisters was terrifying to me. And it must also have been scary for the rest of them because everybody said no, that we are not going anywhere. So, they let us choose.

Hello! Are you doing your job, you know? Are you going to leave it up to the kids? Dumb-ass. I mean. .

Well, anyway, they just left us in the house.

And when I was eleven, my sister Starla started throwing up in the morning. But, she had always occasionally thrown up. Like, toothpaste would always make her nauseous, that sort of thing. I was eleven or twelve.

She had always been heavier than anyone else in the family, but she started gaining weight. And we found out that she was pregnant when she was six months pregnant. She had not had prenatal care, or anything.

She had become good friends with this neighbor, Pat, and my other sister had become friendly with another neighbor, Barbara, who could not stand me.

Anyway, my two sisters went through the court system, and that way got emancipated. At the time, you had to have an adult willing to be responsible for you in order to be emancipated. But, there..... also was that you had to prove there was a problem at home. So, not only did the Social Services workers know there was a problem at my home, but my two older sisters had already been emancipated. There's obviously a pretty big problem, okay? And nobody is going to come in and do anything.

The whole world knew. In my opinion everybody knew. How could you not know?

Starla was. . .it blew me away when she told me that she was pregnant. She came up. . . and she was living at the neighbor's house. And she came over and talked to me. She told me that she was going to have a baby. I asked her who the father was. She was fifteen when she got pregnant.

She said, "It's my fault. I'm not telling, cause it's my fault."

I said, "How could it be your fault."

She said, "I could have said no."

But Raymond E_____, Senior, is the father of my nephew.

My mother,,, when Starla went into labor .... Starla was with me at the house, and she went into labor—her water broke. And I was flipping out. I didn't know what to do. I called my mother at work, and told her that Starla's water had broken.

My mother said, "It's not my problem," and hung up.

I said, "Starla, I will get you to the hospital somehow, if I have to carry you there on my back. I'm not real sure what we are going to do, but...."

So, she went to the neighbor's and the neighbor called my mother and told her, "Look, get your ass home now, or I'm calling the police."

My mother came home, picked Starla up, took her to Baptist Hospital, dropped her off in the parking lot, and then left—just left her standing there.

Then she came home. And when my mother showed up at home, I was, like, "Wha..what's going on," you know?.

She said, "Well, your sister's having a baby."

I said, "What are you doing here? Take me to the hospital. What are you doing here?"

And she got so pissed off at me. I was never allowed to question. None of us were ever allowed to question, anything. You know?

She had just dropped the kid off. How in hell....

She was pissed. She was pissed when we were going through that whole emancipation process, you know. Like, "If you don't want to be my kid. . ."

~ * ~

As I grew older, like I said, I was angry. I was eternally and perpetually pissed off—at everything and everybody.

When I was, like, thirteen, Cliff had a... a heart attack? I think it was a heart attack, or maybe it didn't develop all the way into a full heart attack, as he started having pains, chest pains, trouble breathing and that sort of thing. He had to have a Pacemaker put in.

When he came home from work, the day he had to go to the hospital, he was sitting in a chair, he was leaning over to one side, his head dangling, holding onto his chest. I asked my mother if she was going to take him to the hospital. She said, "No, if he dies, he dies."

I was, like, "I'd hate for anybody to die in my living room. Can you take him to the hospital and let him die there?"

And I don't remember everything about how it happened, but he was sitting in the chair, leaneing over, all slumped over like that, and the truth be told, I didn't have any sympathy for him. Not any at all. I figured that God had finally decided that enough was enough, and, you know, if you are going to die, you're going to die, but don't die in my house. That might sound selfish, but hell, I still believed in ghosts. I was afraid that he would come home and be there forever.

So, at that time, my mother had already been dating Dennis. She called Dennis and told him that Cliff was abusing her, that he had hit her. The man couldn't even get enough air in to stand up, okay? And I'm not saying that to have any sympathy for him, you know. He's got his coming.

But, Dennis, being the kind of man that he was, honestly thought.... But, first of all, he can't be but so good of a man; he was dating a married woman. Okay? I mean, come on. But, it is what it is. He comes over, and he's got a gun. Gets out of his car and he's got a gun!

I went outside, me and my other sister both, and we went, like, "What the hell are you doing with that gun?"

He said ...and my mother was outside... and she said, "Oh, Cliff did this and Cliff did that to me..." And I went, "No, no. The man needs to go to the hospital. You're going to have to get the hell out of here.."

And my mother got mad at us. I didn't realize until later that she was playing both of them. Okay? She waited until Cliff was so weak that he couldn't do anything, and that's when she made her move. And I thought, you know, "That's pretty shitty. You have no balls. You have no backbone whatsoever."

No way. I could see why she wanted to be with Dennis. Dennis is a much better person, but that is, to me, just a nasty way to do it. Just nasty. But the, she was just so damn conniving; she was so self-serving.

That's. . .ah. . ..I really started turning my anger towards my mother at that time—at that age; around twelve or thirteen.

One night, Frank and I were the only ones home. Angela and Starla had already been emancipated. Dean had joined the Air Force so he was gone.

After she split up with Cliff...no, wait a minute. I'm sorry. Let me back up a little bit.

She had already split with Cliff. All the neighborhood kids were at our house, because I remember what a relief it was when he moved out. Nobody was coming in my bedroom any more. Nobody was touching me any more.

Cliff had moved out, because he had found out that my mother was dating Dennis. That's what made him leave. But that wasn't the end of it.

The kids were all playing hide and seek. We were playing with the kid who lived down the road from us, who my sister eventually married. Ward. That was her first husband.

Ward was running to home base and stepped on somebody that was lying in the ditch in front of the house, at the road. Ward jumped over the ditch, and hauled ass to the house.

At first, he thought it was one of us, but then a man stood up and it scared him and he ran to our house, shouting, "Everyone get in the house. Everyone get in the house. Now!"

And this man ran off into the woods. We didn't know what in the hell was going on.

A couple of days later, my mother, Frank and I were the only ones home. And we left. . .we had this back door open. I was sitting on the couch. The door led in from the carport and when you walked inside, the living room was on one side and the kitchen was on the other.

My mother was in the kitchen. I heard a noise outside, under the carport. I went to the door and flipped on the light. We saw a man reaching for the screen door.

The wooden entrance door was open, but the screen door was closed and latched, and the man was reaching for the door handle. The minute my mother saw the man reaching for the door, she slammed the entrance door and locked it.

My mother flipped out and she started telling me that Cliff was trying to kill her, that he had been making threats, and she was like, "Get Frank, get him to the back bedroom and lock the door."

I said, "There ain't no damn way I'm doing that. I ain't going down there without you. You get your happy ass down here with us."

So my mother was fighting me all the way down the hall, and I drug her down the hall, pretty much. We ran around and locked all the windows, and then we ran into her bedroom and locked the door.

We could hear him coming through the bathroom window. The window was kind of high up, and I had a St. Bernard at the time—named him Brett. And Brett wouldn't even let anybody read the electric meter. Okay? And if he didn't know you, you were not coming into the yard. He was mean, too.

But, evidently, this dog knew whoever the person was, because Brett let him come into the back yard, didn't mess with him; didn't even make a sound, not anything. The guy had put a ladder against the back of the house and had climbed through the bathroom window, because we had heard him fall into the tub.

He had cut the telephone lines, so we couldn't call anybody. My mother was loading her gun. She had one. And Frank, I put him in the bed. He was still kind of small. I told him to hide under the covers.

This guy walked down the hall and tried to open the bedroom door. My mother told him, "I've got a gun, If you try to come in here, I'm going to shoot you."

Then he went out of the house, and you could hear him walking. He went out of the house and he came around to her bedroom window. We heard him put the ladder up against the house, and he's climbing up. My mother threw the window open and put her gun in his face, and she said, "Get your ass down from there or I'll shoot you."

So, he jumped down and he ran away.

Well, I went to the neighbor's house and called the police. And the police came out. The ladder was still against the house. They had dogs and all that. Nobody ever found the guy.

And, still today, I honestly believe that Cliff was going to have her killed. I really do. He was going to have her killed.

About a week after that, I was lying in my bedroom. I finally had a room to my self. I was very happy. It didn't dawn on me not to put my bed by the window. I didn't even think about it. It was there all the time. The window was open.

I woke up, and like, I was lying.... my bed went perpendicular to the window. When I woke up and looked up, he was half-way in my window. That man was half-way through my window!

I screamed and.... Was Dennis there that night? Dennis might have been there that night, because when I hit my mother's bedroom door, it was locked. I couldn't get in. And I had Frank with me, 'cause Frank always slept with me. I was screaming and pounding on the door. She opened the door and I told her he was coming into the room, coming through the window.

She went into my room and Dennis was there that night. She went into my room and whipped on the light and saw that the window was open and that the screen was out of the window. The room was empty. Evidently when I had started screaming, he ran. But he had taken the screen out of the window.

The police could never find anybody. We never did know who it was.

It was ridiculous.

I'm certain that Cliff sent the man. I guess he was trying to kill her. I remember that they were going through the custody fight, and all that. And whenever she got with Dennis, Cliff didn't want that. He told her that Dennis didn't want anything to do with six kids.

I said, "Okay, who gets to stay?" Dean was already gone, Angela and Starla had moved out.

Starla had her baby.

And I remember that we moved over to Kerner Road. But, first, I believed that we moved to downtown Kernersville. I'm sorry, I know that I'm disjointed, just rambling, but that's the way my memory is working.

~ * ~

I was dating, and when I was fourteen, I got pregnant. I was still at home. That was before I moved out. I got pregnant and had an abortion. That was before abortion became the safe and sanitary thing it is today.

I hemorrhaged. And my mother would never have found out, but I hemorrhaged. I was bleeding, terribly. And I went downstairs. We were living in a two-story house, at that time. So I went downstairs. She was on the first floor, sewing.

When she moved in with Dennis, every thing changed. Okay? Our background never happened. You know, she just decided that, as long as she didn't admit to it, it didn't happen. Okay? The woman had false teeth from the time she was thirty-five. Dennis didn't find out until they were married. Okay? I mean that kind of stuff.

And I'm the one that told him the truth about her teeth when she pissed me off.

Ah....Well, it's true, you know. I hate that kind of fakeness; I hate it. Don't try to be something you're not.

But..... I went downstairs and I told her that I was bleeding and that I needed to go to the hospital.

I called the guy, okay and told him that I was hemorrhaging and that I was going to have to go to the hospital, and also that I was going to have to tell my mother. He said, "Well, you're not going to tell her by yourself. I'll be there in a minute." He was maybe seventeen, okay? And he came over.

It was a school night so my mother knew as soon as he pulled into the driveway that something was wrong. I let him in the front door. And much to his credit, (now I will give him that much credit) he stood there and he told her what happened, and he said that she (me) needed to go to the hospital.

My mother started raising hell, cussing him out.

I told him just to leave.

And he said, "What the hell? I can't just leave you here. She's going to kill you. I can't leave you."

Dennis told him, "You don't have any choice. You've got to go."

So the boy left. And I went back upstairs. My mother kept saying, "You're not going to the hospital. I don't care if you die. I don't care if you bleed to death," you know, and all this shit.

And Dennis was, "Ah,...no, she's going to the hospital." he said. "We can handle everything else later, but she's going to go to the hospital."

And they had a huge fight over that, because my mother didn't want me to go to the hospital.

And I kid you not, I was bleeding so heavy that .I had soaked a pair of jeans all the way to my knees. That was how bad I was bleeding. And I had gone upstairs to lie down; I was hurting so bad.

And Dennis came up there and said, "Go get in the car."

I was walking down the steps and my mother came out of the kitchen, and said, "Where in the hell do you think you're going?'

I said, "Dennis told me to get in the car."

And she punched me on the side of my head, knocking me down. I saw stars. I came up and I thought, *I'm gonna kill her. I'll kill her right now.*

Dennis had come downstairs and got in between us. She had hold of my hair. Dennis picked me up and was going to carry me out to the car. She kept hold of my hair, and wouldn't let him take me. And she—honestly, in my heart, I believe that if I had died at that time, she wouldn't have given a shit.

And I don't know—I was scared, you know. I knew that I had screwed up. But to me, affection was sex. That was what you did. It had been beaten into me and forced on me until I believed.

She took me to the hospital. Dennis finally told her that, "Look, there's no question. She's going to the hospital. Get in the damn car."

Took me to the hospital and I had to have a D&C. The gynecologist that was on call that night came into the room and I told him that I had had an abortion.

When the doctor walked into the room, my mother was raising hell at me. She was slapping me, you know. He told her that she was going to have to leave. She started raising hell at him, "That's my daughter. I don't have to go anywhere," and all this. And he walked out of the room.

She went back to raising hell with me, I mean, she was just holding me by my hair and slapping me in the face. I had lost so much blood and I was hurting so bad.... The security at the hospital came and told her to leave. They made her leave me alone.

I had the D&C and everything, and I went home. And from that point forward...G,,, it was it was on between my mother and me. It was just on. She just disgusted me. The sound of her voice pissed me off. And I'm sure she felt the same way about me. She felt like I let her down. You know? Everything was about *her*.

And that's when, if there was a drug available, I was taking it. That's when I discovered 'acid'. Loved 'acid'. Absolutely loved it.

Until I found out that, you know, it has permanent effects on your body. "You don't need to be taking LSD, dumb ass!" You know?

Loved it though.

Cocaine? I did cocaine for the first time when I was thirteen. And, like I said, it makes you ten feet tall and bulletproof. I had found it. Found it at a neighbor's house. I knew what it was. I had just never had the guts to do it. You know? So, I picked it up and put it in my pocket. It was an eight-ball. An eight-ball of cocaine. It was a lot... A lot of money. A lot of money that I took that day.

I didn't know how to do it. I didn't know how to cut it. So, I called my girl friend from next door. She came over, and she knew how to cut it. So we took the mirror off my bedroom wall, and cut it out.

And did it. And did it. Did it and did it and did it; all damn day. And I absolutely loved it, I thought, you know. . .and to this day, I kid you not, if it wouldn't kill me, I'd do it every day. I would do it every single day.

Now that's terrible. But, nothing can hurt you. Nothing hurts you.

~ * ~

My mother and I kind of just fell apart after that. You know? Everything I did was wrong; everything she did was wrong. She disgusted me. And so many damn lies.

She got—she got on this kick that I was crazy, that I was mentally unstable.

Damn it. She pissed me off, because I was at the age, or at the point, I guess, where I wanted people to know what had happened to me. I was getting into trouble at school. You know? I had never gotten into trouble at school before, and it was, like, I wanted to tell somebody. I didn't know who to tell. If you looked at me crossways, I was fighting. I mean, you couldn't say anything to me without me going off. 'Cause teenagers usually give parents hard times at that age anyway. This was just double or triple.

~ * ~

Anyway, my mother separated from Cliff, and I guess she got a divorce, because she married Dennis shortly after.

I eventually moved out. I hated my mother. I just hated her. She treated me like dirt after I had that abortion. And I thought, *what a damn hypocrite, because she was pregnant by my stepbrother and had an abortion herself.*

Cliff had an adopted son named Tim. He was the one that died of cancer. When I was eight or nine years old, and to tell the truth, my sister, Starla, would remember more than I, she's older so she would remember when my mother got pregnant. And, there was this huge fight, lots of accusations about Tim.

I walked into the house one time and they, Tim and my mother, were. . .and they jumped apart. . .when I walked in. So, I knew something was going on between them. I don't know what it was, but I know she had an abortion. Because it was at the Wesley Long Hospital. Our next-door neighbor was her nurse. I heard Becky, the neighbor, and my mother talking about my mother's care while she was in the hospital.

You think kids don't pay attention, but they hear a lot.

Yeah, she got pregnant by her stepson, and had an abortion. Yet she treated me like dirt. Just because I screwed up when I was fourteen. And I couldn't get over that.

I couldn't get over the anger. So, the guy I got pregnant with—it was to the point where I would come home and all of my stuff, everything that had been in my room would be on the front lawn. She would just. . .you know. She'd get a wild hair while I was at school and go in and start digging through my room. And, you know, we would start fighting back and forth. She would find a cigarette or something. She kept telling me she was looking for drugs and I'd be thinking, *I'm not stupid enough to leave them here.*

I'd do them before I come home. I'm not going to bring drugs in here. You'd take them from me for yourself!

One time, after an argument, and all my stuff was thrown out the window, the neighbors called the police. And of course they came. And, they didn't believe me. Put me in handcuffs. Because of the lies my mother told them about me, about how bad I was. And of course, the police believed the adult, they always do.

~ * ~

And. . .ah. . .I had a smart-ass mouth. I ..er.. will not lie. I had a smart-ass mouth and I would taunt her, because I was almost as big as she was. And I knew...I had promised myself that one of these days I was going to beat her ass.

The guy that I was dating moved out. The guy .... he got an apartment and wanted me to come live with him. Because I would go to school, and I ..I would seriously have severe bruises, you know? And it was pretty obvious what was going on.

And when I decided I was leaving, I just told her, " I'm done. I can't live here any more. You don't want me here any more."

And she was just, "Fine. Leave. Whatever you want to do."

I went upstairs and started to pack my stuff, and she came upstairs into the room and said, "Oh, no! Everything in here is mine. This belongs to me."

I said, "Well, can I get my clothes? 'Cause you can't wear them, anyway."

And she said, "Yeah, you can take your clothes."

So, I said, "I'll be back tomorrow to get my clothes."

Well, the guy that I was moving in with, his boss (who I eventually married) had a truck. Steve had a truck, and I asked Steve if he would go to my mother's house with me to pick up my clothes. He was, like, "Yeah, I'm neutral, I don't care. If you want to go get your clothes, I'll help you to go get your clothes."

We walked in the house and Steve got halfway up the stairs, and my mother said, "What in the hell are you doing? Who are you? What do you want?'

He said, "I'm just giving her a ride, you know, helping her carry some stuff."

And my mother said, "Like hell! No! You get the hell out of *my* house!"

Steve was, like, "Fine. I'll meet you at the end of the road." meaning at the end of the driveway, because she wouldn't even let him park in the driveway. So, I carried all my clothes out to the truck and moved out.

I was still in high school, working the third shift at (before it became "Prissy Polly's") it was "B & B Kitchen." There was a book binding company behind that building. What they did was, you know, like the cookbooks that have the plastic spirals for a binder? That's what they did, put those binders on books. I got a job there, third shift, getting paid under the table. I was going to school in the morning, and working there third shift.

I did that for about two weeks and then I got called into the principal's office. Mr. Wilhelm was the principal. I was a freshman at East Forsyth. The principal told me that my mother had called the school. Because what she thought was that I would get out of there without her and realize that I couldn't handle it, and then I would be begging her to let me come home.

Well, hell, I had moved out, had an apartment, had a job. I was good; I was fine. You know? I could buy my own dope, smoke it in my living room. And I was happy.

Mr. Wilhelm told me that if I was not living at home with my family, that I couldn't go to school there, or I was going to have to pay tuition. And it was six hundred dollars a quarter. Right? That was illegal as hell—you can't tell a kid that. Okay? So, they made me sign a contract that, if I was not living at home with my mother, because she went to the school and told them that I was just awful, I was incorrigible, I wasn't listening, and of course, he believes the mother, so they made me sign the contract that if I wasn't living home with my mother that I could not go to school there.

So, I moved back home.

Within two weeks, it was on again. I mean, it was flat on. I don't know if. . .it was ridiculous. Because, she thought she had me. And she was pretty upset with me. Anyway, we fought every day, and finally when I came home from school one day, she was, like, "You can't live here anymore."

I said, "What am I going to do about school?"

And she said, "That's your business. That's your problem."

So, I moved out again, and moved in with David, again. And that lasted for. . .God, I don't know. . .about six months, until I decided that's not where I wanted to be anymore. So, we had a big fight and I had to move out of there. I was sixteen years old.

My mother told me I could come back home. Right? So, I moved back home for a little while. Again, that lasted for about two weeks. And then I had to go—again. I moved out of her house, I didn't have anywhere else to go. Angie was living in a one-bedroom house and I called her, and she said........ Chris was living with her, in a one bedroom house, with her and her husband, and she didn't have any room for me. Starla was living with Cliff. Angie told me to call Starla and see if I could stay with her and Cliff.

So I did. I mean, I was on the street; I didn't have anywhere else to stay. And Starla said, "Not tonight. So, I spent about a week, sleeping outdoors in the Fourth of July Park. Then Starla let me come and stay with them. And so I moved in over there.

Within about two weeks time, I woke up and Cliff was in my bed. I had had enough. I'd had enough! I wasn't having that shit no more! I got out of bed. I had always slept fully clothed. I got out of bed and I reached into the closet and pulled out a ball bat and told him that if he touched me again, I was going to beat his head in.

That, of course, didn't go over too well with him. He was telling me, you know, you're so desirable, so beautiful. I remember him saying that and I wanted to vomit! How can you say that to somebody? Ugh, ugh!

Starla had to sleep with him in order to stay there. And he told me that if I was going to stay, I would have to sleep with him, too. "If you don't put out, you can get out!"

I said, "Okay, I'll be gone in two days, because I'm not doing it." So, I packed up my stuff. I called Steve because I was dating him at the time and told him that I had to move.

He said, "Okay, I'll be there in a little while." He came over and put my stuff in his truck and I went to stay with Angie and Ward, for a few days. Then, I moved out with Steve. And I haven't been back since. I was seventeen.

We celebrated my first happy birthday together.

---Starla---

The memories just keep fading in and out. After the birth of my son, I remember there was something about emancipation, but I'm not sure exactly what that is, other than that I was able to move out and get away from my mother. I do know that when you are emancipated, that you must have another adult that will step in and say that they would be responsible for you, if you were under a certain age. I was under that age.

There was a woman who said that she would be the responsible adult. Her name was Pat, and I really loved that woman. But, when I was let out of the hospital with a child, she told me that I could not come and live with them, that there was just no place for me and a child. So, I had no place to go and certainly could not go home to my mother.

In fact, it was absolutely necessary that I get away from my momma. She told me that I could not come home, that she was not going to raise anybody's bastard child, and that I could just take the baby and go anywhere that I could find to live.

At the time that I was discharged from the hospital, I had no place to go. So there I was, just my son, Dale, and me. Thank heaven for Pat. Although she didn't have room for Dale and me, she did have a sister-in-law, Melinda, who would allow me and my son to move into her house, at least for a short while.

We spent several days with Melinda, and that was one of the calm periods of my life. But it didn't last long, as my reputation wasn't exactly shiny.

So, I knew these people who had taken off for the beach. They came back and visited. There was this girl, Fay, who lived at the beach and she said that I could move to the beach with them and live with her. So I said, what the hell, I don't have anywhere to go, so that sounded just great to me.

So I made plans to move to the beach with her. The rest of my family didn't have any room for me, and my momma just didn't give a shit. I wrote to Angie, my older sister. And I called my momma one more time.

I went to work down there and I kept my baby. I don't know why, but there was always something sexual that came up.

I was doing pretty good, but I was living with this family, right? I really enjoyed that time. I would put my baby down and I would play games with him.

I had to go to court, you know, to get emancipated. And Cliff came down to get me. So I came back up here and I go to court, and I'm emancipated. I was going back to the beach to live.

I got back to the beach. There were a couple of kids, and Fay and her husband thought that I was having sex with one or both of the kids. And even with the husband. Anyway, when I got to the beach, he was there and I was told to go down to the pier and see her.

When I got to the pier, which was at a restaurant where we all worked, I found out that I had been framed. I found out that the night I left, someone took twenty-five dollars out of the register, which ain't right. And I think. . .you know. . .this ain't right. I didn't take the money, and she kept on saying, "Well?"

And I'm like, "Did your drawer came up short?" and all this.

And they said, "Yeah."

I knew it was her.

But I was kicked out again.

And I had no place to go. I called my sister, Angie.

~ * ~

Angie talked me into coming back up here and living with Cliff. I didn't want to do it, but I'm not real sure that Angie knew what went on with Cliff and me, but I didn't have a choice. There was only my grandmother who offered to let me live with her, but that really wasn't a choice, since she didn't like me anyway and she hated my son.

Anyway, Angie wanted me to go back to school, and that was alright with me. I had done good when I was younger, and only started doing bad after the sexual shit started with Cliff and his sons. At least those two boys had gone away.

Well, I come up here and I had my baby, and I moved in with Cliff. And. . .ah. . .he kept saying that my son was retarded. My son *is* mentally retarded. We didn't know anything for the first year, not me nor anyone else. But, after a year or so, we noticed that he didn't try to walk, didn't pull himself up, didn't take an interest in anything. And, he would just let his head sag to the side.

I didn't know all of this when I came back from the beach, and then he would have seizures. I thought that he was asleep. Well, I came to find out that he was having seizures.

Well, I was going to school, taking care of my son and Cliff screwed me regularly every night. And my sister was staying there. Angie walked into the room one night and he was on top of me, screwing me. And there was blood in the bed.

Well, me and Angie never talked about it, But.... there were times when I would be mad at Angie because she had to know what the hell was going on, and I was, like, "Help?"

Anyway, Angie was working two jobs; she worked the second shift and the third shift, trying to save enough money so that she would get married. She wanted out of the situation, and I guess she finally did escape.

Then Deena needed a place to stay and had to move in with me and Cliff. My momma wouldn't let Deena stay with her any more. When Deena came to me, I had to tell her that I was sleeping with Cliff. That was hard. I told her that I had no choice. I had no money. And that I had to think of Dale. I told her that I just didn't know what to do.

Deena told me that the two of us could leave, but I was scared and had to take care of my son Dale. Anyway, Deena was dating some guy; I guess it was the one she married. I found out later that Cliff had tried to get to Deena again and had gone to her bed one night. Deena told me that she took a ball bat out of the closet and threatened to beat his fucking head in if he didn't leave her alone. Cliff told her that if she didn't want to let him screw her that she would have to leave, and eventually, she did, moving to stay with Angie.

As for me, I just graduated school but I was still living there, and it got worse. He always wanted me to sleep with him; always wanting to screw or have oral sex. So, like, being in the same bed every frigging night, I went in there but it was hard to sleep. For one thing, my son stayed awake, part of his disease was that he stayed awake about half the night.

I went through hell with my son because he got constipated and he didn't go to the bathroom. He couldn't walk. He couldn't do normal things like little kids do.

Well, I....uh....I finished school. It was really hard on me because, well, because I had a lot of hatred inside of me. And I would fly off the handle with people at school, and shit like that. I would get in trouble. And there was one lady who took an interest in me. She kept me out of trouble.

And, you know, I've never seen the lady again until my brother was....my brother graduated and we went to the Winston-Salem Coliseum. I seen that lady. It made me so happy because I knew she cared. And she still cared. But she quit working there shortly after her husband died. She quit working at East Forsyth.

But we would come and go at Cliff's house. Friends of his would come and go and they knew what the hell he was doing. And we were friends with a guy down the road. Name of Troy. I saw the guy. They tried to drive him crazy. They wanted him gone. And I wanted Cliff gone.

I was in the middle of all this and I tried to commit suicide two or three times. I never made it, never could pull it off.

And. . .uh. . .we got up one morning and I went in the back yard and I saw Troy. There in the back yard, sitting there, holding a paper. And I went down there just to see what was going on and found that he had shot himself in the head. Well, I knew that they had done it to him—drove him to it. But he killed himself.

Well, I had a friend who... I was going to an independent school. She came to me Friday afternoon and told me she was pregnant—with her stepbrother's baby. We were supposed to work on some kind of a program. We were going to make a tape about something from television.

Well, one morning I went to school and I found out that she had shot herself. They said that she had blown her brains all over the place. And they couldn't understand why. Well, they finally found out that she was pregnant, but I never told anybody why—never told them about her stepbrother.

Cliff undoubtedly knew it, and I had no idea why. And that kind of freaked me out.

Well, eventually, my son Dale started seeing a...he started seeing a....well, different doctors and things like that, because he was handicapped. And this guy came out and he brought different things for

Dale to work with, and all. He had seen it. And everybody knew it. Everybody knew that my son was handicapped, his brain affected by the trouble before he was born.

Well, Dale went to a special school, the Northwest Development Day School, and I had to drive him back and forth because there was no bus to take him. And my momma was no help; she was just pushing everybody out of her life. But, I was dedicated to my son.

And there was one woman up there named Gloria. Now she was a nice woman although she was a Mexican. She had adopted a.... what do you call it? Yeah, an autistic boy child that had been abandoned by his mother. The mother had just brought the kid to school and dumped him off and drove away. She never came back.

Gloria really liked Dale, and we became good friends and would go out together. We would go shopping and do other things and we would take good care of Dale.

Well, she....there was this guy that liked me. He was Spanish. And she couldn't figure out why I wasn't seeing nobody.

Well, this guy put a 'hickey' on my neck.

I was, like, "Well, you can't take me home now."

She said, "Why?"

I said, "Because I will get the shit beat out of me. I'll get killed."

I eventually had to tell her the story, all of it. So, she took me out to her house that night. And we lived up in Winston-Salem for a while.

But Cliff called everybody. When I left that night, he called everybody, said that I had left, that I didn't come home and that he was worried, and that it was strange of me.

But, eventually, he found out where I was at. And I had bought...I had bought a..uh.. a truck when I lived with Cliff. I had paid for it with my own money and everything. It was a Bigfoot—a Bigfoot truck. I loved it. We used to stay in it all the time.

Well ..... he wanted the CB radio out of the truck. My son went to school. Cliff stayed after me, hollering that he wanted the CB out of the truck. So, I'm, like, "Okay, I'm bringing the truck down there and you can take the CB out of the truck. And that'll be it!"

Well, I go down there. I go to his house and he takes the CB out. It took him a little while, and I was scared anyway. And I kind of stayed on my side of the truck, stayed away from him. And ....then, I was driving....uh....my brother was staying at the fire station right down the road. And so, I had been to his house and I had been to the fire department. Then I started coming back to Winston.

Well, I noticed these detectives. I knew they were police, I mean, this is. . . I just knew it. Well, I got ready to turn down the street that I lived on. Wha... they pulled me over. They were, like. . .they used sponsor detectors on me and it was like, "I ain't smoked any marijuana then. I didn't do anything, I'm clean!"

They said, "We got a phone call from Communications that said you've got a bag of 'weed' in that truck and you're going to deliver it to a bunch of Mexicans."

Which, it was Spanish people that I lived with. Well, Gloria's son pulls up; I hadn't even met her son yet. I didn't know who he was, but he knew who I was. And he was hollering for me and hollering at me, and that looked even worse because he was Spanish.

Well, I said, "There's nothing in that truck."

And they are, like, "Well, can we look?"

I'm like, "There ain't nothing in my truck."

He said, "Do you want to bet?'

I said, "Yeah!"

He goes under the side of the truck, went right to it, and found a bag of 'weed'. Well, I went to jail.

They came to try to get me out of jail, but they weren't going to get me out of jail because I was underneath bond that was outrageous.

For the weed that wasn't even mine, they took my truck. And I stayed in jail for a couple of nights.

Cliff knew he had done it. And I knew he had done it. And he got it from his son, who was dealing in drugs at the time.

And...ah... my momma eventually bonded me out, but she told me that I had to pay back the money. And she also knew that Cliff had done it.

I eventually got charged with it. And when it came through, Cliff paid for the lawyer, and he got a lawyer that was on *his* side. And I kept trying to tell these people that I was getting messed with and that I was in an abusive situation. They kept... The D.A. kept saying that I was on drugs and that I was running away from home. And I don't understand, because I was old enough to be on my own. I was emancipated and everything. And I couldn't figure out why they were saying that I was trying to run away from Cliff, and that I was a teenager that was out of control.

But, I wasn't. I hadn't. . .I never smoked weed until I was. . .uh... God. Uh. . .I had Josh. I've got two boys. It was way after I had Josh. They're six years apart. So you can imagine. I waited until I was.... well, twenty-something years old. Then I started smoking pot.

But...you know, they fooled me, because I couldn't understand how the D.A. even got me. And they made me pay these fines and I had to pay my momma and them back. And it was stra ..... he even took it all the way up to a jury. So I was in front of people. They convicted me of something that I didn't do.

Now I had a felony put on my record. Then the son-of-a-bitching D.A.... I was working at Exxon on...uh...Stratford Road in Winston. He comes in, the next god durn morning. Now, I want to come over that counter and knock the hell up out of him. And I felt like that he got in my face because he got me.

Well, I am trying to tell you the best I can. . .you know that my memory is playing tricks on me, skipping here and there. Remembering just in bits and pieces.

But, there was a time that I told my momma that I was trying to get away from Cliff and that I wanted my brothers and sisters back. I told my momma what was going on with me and Cliff, but I think she already knew it. She didn't care. She lived with Dennis at the time and suggested that I come over there and live.

But when I got over there, she wasn't helping me, or nothing. She wouldn't help me with a ride to get my son to the school. And he was handicapped. I was trying everything in the world. But I couldn't figure it out. How had he come to be handicapped? And I tried everything that I could, trying to get him back and forth to school. My momma didn't help me a bit. So, I ended up moving back in with Cliff, because I wanted Dale to go to school. My son was more important than I was.

So I moved back in with him, but that was before I finally went back to Winston. But, yeah, my momma knew what was going on. And I felt like—I was sad. Real sad.

My momma could get inside my head quick. But Deena started taking up for me. She went to the court with me and everything.

When I lived with Gloria, I met a Mexican named Salvador. We hit it off pretty good and I got pregnant by him. I didn't want to have another baby without being married, so Deena and them planned a wedding that would be held in my brother's back yard. I married Salvador, but he wasn't the kind of a husband that would make a family. He would go out and drink all night, drinking up all of the money that we had.

I wound up selling drugs while working at the Royal Cake Company, trying to make enough money just to feed my son and me, and Salvador, since he wouldn't work none at all.

I don't know where he is now. I guess that we are still married. He got so many DUI's that the government finally deported him back to Mexico. Who knows? Maybe he's one of those illegal aliens and has married some other women. It would be just like him.

It was while I was working at the Royal Cake Company that I met Sandra. Sandra introduced me to 'crack' and let me tell you, it will mess you up. I was doing 'crack' heavily and Sandra had convinced me that I was meant to be a lesbian. I thought I was in love and that I had finally found a situation where I wouldn't be used and abused.

Sandra was just as abusive as any man; she would push me around, slap me, and take my money. I never had anything. And I couldn't give up the 'crack', at least, I couldn't until I found out that my grandmother had died. That really shook me up; I had loved my grandmother.

Anyway, finally Sandra became so bad that I needed help. I called Deena, and she promised to come and get me. She did, but she brought a gun. She said later that she didn't know what kind of weirdoes would be hanging around Sandra, and that she felt better with the gun.

Deena told Sandra that if she didn't leave me alone that, "I'll blow your fucking head off. I'll shoot your fucking ass! You fucking crack-head!"

I guess Sandra believed her, because I only heard from Sandra once or twice after that, and then Deena called her on the telephone and repeated her threat. After that, Sandra just disappeared.

I found out later that Deena had been drinking and didn't want a DUI. She had a friend, Carey; a friend of Deena's who was driving with her and had not realized that Deena had a gun. And when she came to King, which is where I was living with Sandra, and pulled out the gun, Carey shit a brick. He was also very quiet on the trip back to Winston.

Things began to improve a little when I met Lynn. She had been working with Deena, cleaning houses. We were all doing alright, and I was really in love with Lynn. I think she thought the same about me. But, about that time, I was in an automobile accident. I was in a truck and the truck rolled over, hurting my back, and making it impossible for me to work.

After that, I don't remember much of anything clearly; it is almost as if I was in a fog for a long while. The medicines and pills that the doctors gave me to ease the pain ate into my brain. And I would take a lot of them. I don't know what it means, but the doctors found out during this time that I was 'skitzo' or something like that. Anyway, they just gave me more pills for that.

Then, the funniest things began to happen. There was a voice in the ceiling fan, and he would talk to me. He told me that he had seen a police officer come into my house and change the dates on my calendar. When I got up, I looked at the calendar and found out that the ceiling fan was right—the dates had all been changed. Even the hot air vents and the grills agreed that the police had been there and had changed the dates. I called Deena and told her about it, but I don't think that she believed me.

Lynn and me were breaking up one day and together the next day, then breaking up again. I was living in a trailer that I had bought, but now that I wasn't working, I was having trouble making payments. I was due to have a settlement with the insurance company about the truck accident, but they kept stalling and I was in danger of losing my trailer. My momma was always hanging around, waiting for the insurance settlement, but I decided that she wasn't going to get any of it, cause she didn't help me.

I called Deena, and she helped for a while, holding off the trailer people, until it was just not possible to hold them off any longer. So they took the trailer. Before I lost the trailer, I slipped in the shower and fell. I called Deena and I guess that I called my momma also, because when I woke up, she was there as was the Emergency Medical Team.

We moved in with Deena, Josh and me. It was a shit-hole of a trailer, but it was better than being on the street. I didn't mind, at least as long as the pills held out. They made everything fuzzy but that was okay. I found out later that when I had fallen in my trailer, my mother had cleaned out everything of value, the television set and the earrings that I had inherited from my grandmother. I never saw those items again. The only thing that I asked of Deena was that there would be no men, no men of any kind.

She was dating a shit-head named Roy at the time, but she kept him away from us. I remember Roy because one Christmas Eve, my momma and a friend went to Deena's trailer and used toilet paper to roll Roy's pick-up truck. They left me at momma's house.

I found out when Deena called my momma and told her to get over there and clean it up. My momma lied and said that she didn't know anything about it. Deena said that she was going to call the police and I guess that she did because when my momma took me home and dropped me off at the end of the long driveway that led to the trailer, I saw Deena talking to the sheriff.

I don't remember it myself, but Deena said that I ran down that long driveway to her trailer and that I later threatened to kill her two different times. I don't think I did, but I was taking a lot of narcotics,

Nurantan, Suriquil, Oxycontin and other stuff. I don't know what they are, or even if I am saying them right, but there was a lot of pills and I was taking them all. Eating them like candy.

On New Year's Eve, Deena came home from working eight hours. She worked in collections. When she got home, she was angry because Josh and I were sitting on the couch in shorts. Josh always kept the heat low, but I wanted to be warm. I tried to tell Deena that I was cold, but she wouldn't listen, screaming about an electric bill of two hundred dollars a month. She was yelling like a bitch, so I picked up a can of corn and threw it at her. It missed, but she said that we had to go. And on New Year's Day, she made us leave.

I moved in with Chris but that didn't last too long, only a couple of months. Chris was having trouble with his kidneys. He had a lot of stones, as many as one hundred on one side and about the same on the other. He had to be in the hospital about every two months to have stones removed. That made it impossible for him to keep a job, and as a result, was losing his trailer.

We butted heads, Chris using my truck to go to work. My momma was still pushing, scheming, trying to get a part of my insurance settlement that I was going to get. Chris and I got into it, sometimes violently physical. One day, my mother said that Chris had suffered two broken ribs, and that I would need to move out.

She helped me move into what's called a safe house. That's a place where battered or abused women are offered living quarters. Chris moved into a place behind Angie's house. My momma and I broke into Chris's place while he was away and we cleaned out everything. At least, we took everything of value. And Chris knew who had done it. There had been a witness.

Chris filed a report with the police and everything and he even pressed charges. I admitted the truth and gave back to Chris everything that I had taken and he dropped the charges. Even dropping the charges against my momma, although she continued to lie and say that she had not been there.

The place for battered women changes locations from time to time, being at different addresses so as to protect the women. I had to move from one to another, and my momma helped me. I didn't know until later, but my momma robbed the place blind, stole everything she could, all the pictures, sheets, blankets and anything else that wasn't nailed down. When I found out, I wanted to make things right. When I finally got my insurance settlement, I donated seven hundred dollars to the battered woman's organization to help repay what my momma had stole.

I don't really hate my momma, despite all that she has let happen to me and Deena. But Cliff? That was a different matter, as he always kept coming around after me all the time when we were young, and even after my first son was born. There were times when I had no money, not a penny, and could not feed my son, and I had to move in with him, and you know what that meant. If I wanted to stay there, I had to be a,,,,. willing to screw, at any time.. Not that I wanted anything to do with that nasty, slimy bastard, but it was the only way. Only this time I knew a little more. I made sure that my son was well fed, but another problem jumped up.

My oldest son suffered a mental deficiency and even now in his adulthood, he has to remain in a mental facility. Just when you thought you had seen it all, it is now evident that some sadistic bastard at the mental hospital had raped my son, over and over.

Is there a God? Hah!

That time that Deena moved in with me and Cliff, she was having it rough, and needed a place to stay. At first I couldn't let her but then Cliff relented and allowed her to move in with us. I found out later that Cliff told Deena that if she wanted to stay, she would have to sleep with him and give him a blowjob. Deena moved out and I was left with Cliff. I really wanted to get away, but I didn't have any money, and couldn't get a good job. Besides, I had a son to take care of, so I just put up with anything Cliff wanted to do. I mean, what else could I do?

At the time that I married the man by the name of Salvador, I'm not sure whether I actually loved him, or just saw him as a way to get away from the vicious people that were surrounding me. Another son was born, and has now become a somewhat normal young man. Unfortunately, he had also suffered from the abuse and havoc that was visited upon his mother before his birth.

Taking care of a handicapped son wasn't easy, and I believe that I did the best I could under the circumstances, but first my abused childhood, and then an abused housewife. I didn't know there were so many sick sons-of-bitches in the world. There very well may have been some fine men in the world, but as a child, I never met a single one. At least, not one that I can remember. They were all after the same thing. I grew to hate men. In fact, thanks to being virtually abandoned by my mother, I grew to hate everyone.

My younger son Joshua got into trouble. He just wouldn't go to school nor follow any of the rules. He began selling drugs and doing other things, and finally wound up at a wilderness camp. It was good for him. That's where you live outside, and work. You have to grow the food you eat and live like they used to live in the mountains or on the frontier. He is still having problems, but has been learning a lot of discipline, which was more than I could teach him.

I was still living in King, in my own trailer, when I kept hearing someone outside trying to break in. I just knew it was Cliff, trying to get me again. I called Deena and she drove to King, but couldn't find anybody. It happened over and over.

One night, Deena told me that I was going to have to go to the Dorothea Dix Facility and be tested. She thought that the drugs had begun to affect my brain. I didn't think so, but she and Angie threatened to take my two sons away from me unless I went. So, I agreed.

If you have never been inside a crazy house, let me tell you that there are really some crazy people in there. Real crazy. I got my eyes opened when I saw what really crazy people are like. They are weird—de...er..disaraanged.

I saw Michael Hayes when I was in there. You remember Michael Hayes? The Salisbury Road killing where seven people died? He was there. He was in this clear cell. Actually, the clear cell was surrounded by another clear cell, sort of like a cell within a cell. In the perimeter between the two cells, there were guards stationed there. Armed guards. Guess they didn't want him to get out.

That freaked me out. Scared the shi... scared me to death.

And then there was this girl who climbed into bed with me. That was nice, someone to love me. But, those bastards soon found that out and they stopped it.

The doctors began giving me medicine and testing me. I don't know what they found out, but the medicine made life a little easier. The medicine also made George a little easier to get along with.

You know George, don't you? He's that strange guy that has a nest in my head. He's always there. He is the man of the house. But, he is a mean, mean man. He doesn't want to have sex with me, but he hides things from me. He will take my teeth out of my mouth and hide them; makes it hard to eat. And he will hide my money, my trailer keys, and all that. Eventually, when he is finished playing or tormenting me, he may bring those things back—sometimes. He usually puts my teeth where I can find them, but he doesn't always let me find the money and the other stuff. Guess he spends it on himself, but I don't know what he spends it on.

But anyway, things are better now. Thanks to the insurance settlement and thanks to Deena and the man they put in charge of my money. They didn't let Cliff or my momma get any part of it. That's good. They helped me find a place of my own, and it's paid for so I won't get kicked out. And I don't have to have anybody live with me. Not even a girl, although

I still believe I was always supposed to be a lesbian. And certainly there ain't no damn man.

~ * ~

My daddy did come back around and live with me for a while. He moved into the basement where I stayed. How it came about was that I found out that he was in Las Vegas and went to get him and have him move in with me. His wife, Diane, came with him.

He was in bad shape, fat and old with lots of problems. He had never worked; nor had Diane, although eventually she found some sort of job.

There was a half-brother who got a job and a half-sister that I enjoyed talking to. She helped me take care of Joshua, sometimes. She would serve as a babysitter sometimes.

But my daddy said that he just couldn't make it here and that he was going back to Las Vegas. I don't know why, he couldn't make it there either, but there was no holding him back.

Chapter 5

---Deena---

Steve and I got married two days before I turned twenty.

When I was seventeen, everything just came crashing down on me. Like I said, I was so flipping angry; angry with everyone and everything; angry at myself, angry at my life, angry at the world. And so .....everything just built up over the years. I was so pissed off. I hated myself. I hated life. But Steve saved me; he is the one who convinced me to go to counseling at the age of eighteen. Honestly, if I hadn't done that, I'd have killed myself.

I wanted to stay with Steve; after all he was the only one who seemed to care at all for me. I was glad to marry him. Sort of pay him back, you know, make him happy. He really was the first person that gave a shit about me as a person.

Steve is probably always going to be one of my best friends. He held my hand, stood beside me when everything was tough on me, you know. He didn't have it so great, himself. And I knew that he would be a good daddy, because his dad wasn't a very good dad. And he was determined to make sure that …… whatever children he had would have a good father. To me that was the most utmost important thing; to make sure that if I ever had a child that the child was well taken care of, and that part of Steve was very attractive to me; *very attractive* to me.

So, we got married, and we were married for almost five years before we had a child. My son was planned, my son was wanted, my son was—you know—my son was everything I wasn't. My son came home to a beautiful nursery. And he had two caring parents who doted on him. I guess you could say that we may have spoiled him a little. No, not a little; a lot. But that's okay.

Steve and I are divorced now. Not because we were not friends. We had begun to argue. . .eh. Sorry I kind of choked up there. Steve is a good guy. Steve is a great guy.

But I have a drive; I've always had a drive, a hunger that has never been satisfied. I can't just sit back and wait for someone to take care of me. That's not my way. That didn't work and never had worked. So, I believed, and still believe now, that if I want it, I have to try to get it. Myself. Not the best attitude in a wife, and not the best medicine for a marriage, but that's the way it is. Steve was nowhere as aggressive or as pushy as I, and that is what caused friction, that eventually led to the divorce. I was willing to shovel shit to get ahead or to get what I wanted or needed. Steve wanted to start at the top and get there without toil or trouble. But, that's him. And that's his way.

But, we are still good friends today.

Personally, I know that I have come a long way. I believe that I've almost got my life together. Not quite there yet, but well on my way. I have always been able to earn a living for my son and myself. It's not that Steve hasn't chipped in to help provide for our son when he could, but I've never wanted alimony; I don't want anything for free; not food stamps; not welfare; not even a handout. I felt that if I wanted anything I could earn it, if I was given the chance.

The trouble I was experiencing at home eventually led to trouble at school and that finally led to me having to take entry-level jobs. Of course, my strong work habits and drive would soon move me above the entry-level job. It did at AMP, where I started working when I was nineteen, and it did at John Deere at a later time.

But, things are better now and getting better day by day. Now, I have a future, a definite future, thanks in a large part to the people I'm with now. I have had the time to resume my studies and I'm much less than a year away from my college degree. That degree will allow me to have a reasonably decent income, regardless of what else may happen or may have happened in my life.

And, for the first time—the very first time—I am comfortable with myself. Yes, I still have a lot of anger; anger at Cliff, anger at my mother, and anger at society. But not the fiery hot, blazing rage of earlier years. For the most part, I have learned to live with it, and with the help of those around me who love me for myself; it is becoming minutely easier every day.

As to Cliff, he is still out there—free and alive. Sure, I'd like to see him get what's coming to him. And I'm sure that somewhere and sometime, in this life or the afterlife (yes, I'm a believer), Cliff will get his just deserts. And out there also is my mother; my failed protector. And may God forgive me, and despite the counseling, and in spite of all of the good advice given me from pastors and priests, from people I know and love and respect, I still just can't forget.

Yes, I still am filled with hatred for both of them. It doesn't seem possible that I will ever forgive them. And if I could pardon them for what has happened to me, I could never forgive those animals for what has happened to my sister, Starla.

Why would a grown man do such thing to innocent babies?

Why would a caring mother ignore what was happening?

Why?

Can there be a loving God?

~ * ~

Don't feel sorry for me. Don't you dare feel sorry for me! Actually, my life is far better now than I ever thought it would be. I am able to survive on my own, meet people on my terms, and I know who and what I am and what I am worth.

And don't feel sorry for my sister, Starla. She is in her own world, a world where nothing threatens and a world where the people around her are there to help.

If you have any feelings, feel pity for those young children out there who are going through much of the traumatic experiences that Starla and I suffered. And, if you feel enough pity, perhaps you'll get off your ass and do something that will cause incest, perhaps the most vile of all sins, to cease and to allow our children—yours and mine—to grow up in a world where love lives and lust fades away.

Before I end my story, I want to say something to all of the innocent little girls and the innocent little boys out there who are being molested. It's not you. I understand. Maybe your mothers or your fathers don't believe you, but I know. It's not your fault. You are not to blame. You should not let adults make you think differently. Don't let them put their shame on you. They are the evil ones. They are the evil ones. They are the monsters. It's not you. If you need help, go to your teacher, your school principal, a preacher, the stranger on the street, a man or woman in the store, or a policeman—anyone. Don't believe for a moment that you are bad, that you are wrong. It's not you. It's *them*. I know.

And if they don't believe you, just keep telling them, over and over and over and over. Don't stop. Don't ever stop. Someone, somewhere will hear you. Someone will help.

God bless.

---Starla---

Daddy didn't make it in Las Vegas this time either. His health was too bad and Diane wasn't much help either. They took off to Idaho, leaving a lot of stuff in storage. I guess they thought that they would make out.

Somehow, I knew that I would never see daddy alive again, and I was right. I never did see his eyes again. In fact, I never did see him at all. When he died, and they called to let me know that he had died, I refused to believe it. I didn't want to believe it.

"That's not true!" I remember crying. "He can't be dead."

For the longest time, I believed that he was alive even though 'George' kept telling me that Daddy was dead. I just didn't believe him, but he continued to tell me, day after day, night after night. Finally, I had to accept the truth. My daddy was dead and I didn't even have the money to go to his funeral.

'Bye, daddy.

Antilog

I was sitting here, very late in the night, putting these last thoughts into words. Remembering the pain, the anguish, and the horror that filled Deena's voice and sobs, as she tried, with enormous difficulty, to relate as much as she could of what she could remember.

Recalling Starla's inability to talk without slurring her words, her not being able to think clearly, able only to remember the grisly details of the sexual predators who stalked the two young children. And still, the dimly remembered pain causing copious tears to flow.

As hard as it was for me to hear all of the shocking details, it had to have been a thousand-fold more difficult for them to tell what happened, how each of them was used and abused.

Although Deena has come to know and accept that what happened was no fault of hers, still, talking about the events to anyone, especially a man, a man who is going to record each slimy act by despicable grown men and women, has to be more gut-wrenching than is imaginable. I'm glad that she had the strength to get her life back on track.

I wish the same could have been true for Starla. But, maybe she's better off as she is.

~ * ~

Even at the very beginning, with the first few words, I was absolutely certain that I didn't really want to write this difficult book. I feared that if I agreed to do so, I would hear things that I didn't want to hear. Learn evil things that I didn't want to know. Still, I had served in the military, and had spent time in France, and in Paris, there is a place called Rue Pigalle—a street where you can find almost anything you can imagine. So, I didn't expect to be overwhelmed by the depravity visited by adults on their own children.

Does the word 'disgust' mean anything to you?

The evil manipulations of the young baby girls by their own family—disgust is not strong enough. I don't know of a word in any of the languages I have studied that is strong enough to describe the feelings generated toward the men that perpetrated these depraved actions on young, innocent, unsuspecting children and the adult women who buried their head in the sand and pretended not to be aware.

Can you find any sympathy for them?
Are these people sick, depraved or what?
How can anyone. . .?

~ * ~

Now, I'm sitting here once again at my computer, putting the last few sentences of this book together. Although I had given up on trying to rationalize why I was so determined that this book be published, I believed I had finally figured out the reason why I was driven to complete this book. It wasn't greed, nor even the urge to expose evil people to the world. Perhaps it could be another step in the healing process of abused children.

But suddenly, the last straw fell, my senses began to operate and I finally understood.

The straw?

Today, on the news broadcast, the police of Durham, North Carolina announced that they had arrested the mother of five children for soliciting sex from two undercover policemen. Not for herself, but for her seven year old daughter. That's right. Seven-years-old. And Mom is soliciting, offering her young daughter for pornographic pictures and anything else, including sexual activities if the price were right.

My God!

And this was not a destitute minority single parent, or even a wayward impoverished individual or an alien immigrant. The media portray these types of people as ones most likely to stray.

No, this was a supposedly normal woman, the reputable mother of several children. Why in God's name?

Okay, maybe she was hurting. Or perhaps she needed the money for housing or for food or for medicine. It could have been that she even needed it for her children. But then, why didn't she just do it herself; spread her legs, or her cheeks, or her lips. Surely, after five children, she knew how to do it and what to do.

But, no, it had to be her daughter. Seven years old. Not even old enough to know what sex is, and her mother. . .

Okay, I have frequently mentioned God's name. For one long, agonizing moment, I thought about what I would do if I were God. I believe I'd take one long last sad look at this earth and these people that He had so lovingly created after His own image. Then, if I were God, I would likely break my promise. I would take my rainbow out of the clouds, and I would turn the faucet on. However, this time, no warning. No Ark. No two-by-two. Demolish everybody and everything.

Sure, I might have to start the whole process all over, but I wager the next people would be better. They surely couldn't be worse.

Then I had a different and scary thought. Maybe we, you and I, are being tested—to check us out. Frankly, I don't believe I have earned a gold star. How about you?

All right. Now it's clear. I know why I wrote this book. Love. Respect. Love for children who are faced with such monsters. Respect for anyone who can undergo such a horrific, traumatic childhood and emerge as a sane, whole being.

And outrage!.

Outrage—sheer, unbridled fury. Not Deena's anger. I didn't and couldn't take any of those burdens away from her. She still has her full share of rage.

Rather, she reached down deep inside me and lit my own lamp of anger; ignited my own emotions. It is a created outrage at the thought that these monsters are out there in the world. Free from any punishment, from any vengeance. Free to continue to do it, and to do it again and again.

And I'm not writing with Starla's anguish. The demons that torment her even to this day dominate and control her every thought, her very actions. There is no peace for her, no escaping from 'George.'

I said in the beginning I wouldn't place blame, but I find that I must. How could I do otherwise? How could anyone?

But, now the world will know that "*they*" are out there. And the world will know who *they* are.

And now, you know. *They*, and many, marny others like them, are out there, somewhere. Perhaps, even somewhere close, close to you. *They* may be your neighbors. Or, *they* may your friends. Or, *They* may be your relatives, someone hidden in your own family..

What are you going to do?

One last comment to Bill O'Reilly should he ever read this. And to another outspoken celebrity: Oprah Winfrey. And to others: to Dr. Phil, Nancy Grace, Glenn Beck, Larry King, Ellen DeGeneres, Neal Boortz and to the many noted spokespersons of the same ilk who shape and help form public opinion; champions all of various causes.

It's not really a complete secret. You know what is happening to our children—our babies. Doesn't this offend you? Do you really think that Jessica's Law is severe enough? Can't we just put these monsters away forever and ever? Lock them away so they will never have a second chance to attack our young, our innocent children?

How about if we resurrect Alcatraz? You know, that infamous prison from which there was no escape. Perhaps if we take all of the sexual predators and lock them up there together with all of the sex maniacs and rapists that are in the U.S. prison system and then take away all of the guards, they might get exactly what they deserve. Don't you think?

Should we also take away all of their food? But then all the do-gooders will yell about the prisoners rights!

In your own words, "What say you, Bill?" How about you, Oprah? Dr. Phil? Ellen? Glenn?

Nancy? Larry? Neal? And the rest of you: the "Movers and Shakers" of public opinion?

You may be of the opinion that the of your name is a tawdry attempt to use your fame to sell more books. Well, yes, that very may well be true—at least, in part. But it's for a good cause, not a tawdry one. The primary purpose of Deena and Starla's effort is to galvanize public opinion and to demand action to stop this evil crime against nature.

Anyway, the net proceeds from this book are going to a foundation to help counsel victims of childhood incest.

If you, and we, the people-collectively join together behind any just cause, any cause at all, the resulting public outcry would force the non-caring public officials and soft judges to become the steadfast defenders of personal safety that the Constitution has promised even the youngest child.

How long will your conscious allow you to stand mute while this evil ravages our innocent children? Haven't you had enough? Are you ready for this greatest of challenges?

Are your fiery steeds ready? Are your lances still sharp? Can't you hear the call?

Codicil

From Deena

A personal word. I have finished reading what Poppa Owensby has put to paper, and just had to add my two cents. Frankly, reading the horrific story of my sister was at least as painful as reading my own, if not more so. And I assure you, reading my own word and those of my sister has to be one of the more painful experiences of my life. In some way, reading those terrible words was as bad, or worse, than when I telling Jack the ghastly details about my life. It's hard, seeing everything down in black and white and learning about the depths of depravity that were visited on Starla. Even so, during the period of time of relating those occurrences to Jack and then reviewing his manuscript, there is something missing; something incomplete, something vital.

You've learned a little concerning my sister Starla's situation. She remains permanently disabled, unable to work. Having received a reasonable settlement from the insurance company that has been invested and, despite the swirling economy, she won't lack for housing, food or care for the rest of her life. Being heavily impaired by the traumas she has experienced and the copious intake of drugs that she has partaken since her early teens, Starla is in a world of her own, a world where there is little realization of reality. So, in her own way, she's content within herself.

As for me, I've changed. Even from the person when Jack and I began this saga. I have learned, or perhaps the word should be *realized*, that there are some good people out there; good men and good women. Very good people, but not necessarily perfect people. Many, even most people have good points, but also have a few flaws. And, if you are going to be a part of the here and now, you must learn how to look for the good.

One of the good people that I've identified was Steve, my first (and so far only) husband. We didn't divorce because he was a bad person, and the parting was rather friendly. I still think of him in a good way, while realizing that he, like myself, does have a few thorns. Still, it was Steve who was there just when I needed someone and, thanks to his caring, I am alive and growing as a person.

I've met other good people, including the man I'm going to marry. With his help, his encouragement and his support, I've been able to realize a life-long dream, and return to school. I graduated college this summer, and couldn't have done it without his caring and urging. He and my son were both rooting me on, and so was his family. All were supportive, encouraging and praising, helping me to realize that I too am a good human being, helping me grow, helping me overcome. So there's a lot of love there, they actually believe in me. And love is good.

And, that's it, that is what is missing. Thus my message to you, the reader.

Incest is the most prevalent sexual abuse crime in the world. You wouldn't think so, not here in the good old United States. But it is. U.S. residents don't all wear white hats. They are not all totally good. And neither are the members of our families. Mine or yours.

Still, there's something more. Not everyone is a sexual pervert. Not everyone is a child molester. But, there are a lot of them out there. I'm not a shrink, and this is just a guess, but I believe that the ones who are molesters of children are truly mentally deranged, at least in this one area. The person may otherwise be a perfectly normal father or mother, sister or brother, aunt or uncle. The person may never drink, curse, beat a dog, or even exceed the speed limit. The person may go to church every week, pray and participate, donate funds to charities. Still, in this one area, that person is mentally deranged. Nothing else could explain why adults would attack children.

No, it's not the sex drive. No, it's not because the violator wants to make the child feel good. It's something inside the mind of the individual that drives him, or her, to sexually molest a child, even an infant. Perhaps when the psychiatrists finally discover why a grown adult would force sex on a young child, steps can be taken to prevent such actions. Maybe.

In the meanwhile, what about the hundreds of thousands of you who have been molested? Are you forced to hide the secret from others? Because of fear of scandal or rejection? Do you have troubled dreams, nightmares, or problems with your emotions? Has your child come to you or seem to be hiding things from you?

You know, there is help. Counseling certainly helped me a lot. It has helped many others, as well. Counseling helped me to understand that what happened to me was not my fault. It wasn't me. In fact, I had nothing to do with it. What happened was that a sick man, in fact several sick people, used and abused me. But that wasn't me. That wasn't my fault. It didn't make me a bad person. That was on them. And because it was not my fault, I share no blame. Blameless, innocent as a lamb. Can you understand that? Can you accept that? Believe it, it's true. Excuse me? No! No way, not if you're the abuser, I'm not trying to find an excuse or an explanation for you. In fact, in my mind, you don't even exist, except for being a vile blot on humanity. Admittedly you may be sick, but surely you know the right from the wrong. You made the choice.

But. if you are a victim, take heart. Statistics say that one in every six females is sexually assaulted before she reaches the age of eighteen. And one of every ten males is sexually assaulted before he reaches the age of eighteen. You may be shocked that than sixty-five percent of the assaults are by a relative or a close friend. Yeah, I know. Some friend. And some relative. No, on the other hand, you probably won't be shocked, you may well be one of the unfortunate ones that learned the truth the hard way.

So, now, how about you? Can you cope? Can you accept the truth that it's not your fault, that you are still a good person? And can you understand that there are good people out there to help you? So, go ahead. Tell them. Tell your mommy. Tell your daddy. Tell everyone. Don't hide it. Don't be ashamed. Let them know the truth.

Parents! Can you accept the truth? If your child comes to you, are you just going to brush off what they are saying, are you going to really listen, trying to understand, trying to believe? Can you believe it? You might as well. Odds are that it's the truth.

I guess, in my own way, I'm trying to tell all of you fellow victims out there that I understand, that you are not alone, that there are hundreds of thousands, or even millions of us. Yes, I am one, and so is Starla. But, thank God, it wasn't our fault, we were not bad people, we are not bad people, and we can't let the bad people win. If we hang our head in shame, if we accept any part of the shame, if we continue to hide the truth from our families, from the authorities, and from ourselves, the bad people win.

Above everything else, regardless of what religion that you believe in, or even if you don't believe, there is some supreme being...call Him—or Her—God or whatever...that supreme being made you. And God don't make junk.

We survived it, my sister and I. Each in our own way, sure, but we survived it. And we're continuing to grow. If I could, I'd shout it from the highest mountain, from the tallest building, from the sky itself.

Lift up your head. Lift up your spirit. Look the world right in the eye. Be proud of who you are. You too can survive. You can grow.

Now, I've said all that I can say.

See you.

      Deena

www.ingramcontent.com/pod-product-compliance
Lightning Source LLC
Chambersburg PA
CBHW070556100426
42744CB00006B/298